THE RIVERINA *Runs* THROUGH MY BLOOD

By Graham S. Robb

NENGE BOOKS, Australia

The Riverina Runs Through My Bood

Copyright © Graham Robb 2018

The right of Graham Robb to be identified as the author of this work has been asserted by him in accordance with the Copyright Amendment (Moral Rights) Act 2000.

All rights reserved. No part of this book may be reproduced, distributed, or transmitted in any form or by any means, including photocopying, recording, or other electronic or mechanical methods, without the prior written permission from the publisher, except in the case of brief quotations embodied in a book review and certain other noncommercial uses permitted by the Australian Copyright Act 1968 (the Act) allows a maximum of one chapter or 10% of this book, whichever is the greater to be photocopied by any educational institution for its educational purposes provided that the educational institution (or body that administers it) has given a remuneration notice to the Copyright Agency Limited (CAL) under the Act.

Published by Nenge Books, Australia, 2018
ABN 26809396184
email: nengebooks1@gmail.com
www.nengebooks.com

Cover design: Cynthia Bacon
Cover photograph: Graham Robb
Title font: https://pixelbuddha.net/freebie/breathe-font-free-download
Desktop and layout: Nenge Books

The National Library of Australia Cataloguing-in-Publication data:
Author: Robb, Graham
Title: The Riverina Runs Through My Blood

Nenge Books specialises in publishing small runs of quality books using cost effective print-on-demand technology, and welcomes enquiries to assist in publishing biographies and other publications in both printed and ebook form.

ISBN 978-0-6482882-0-6

Also available as an ebook ISBN 978-0-6480675-8-0

I wish to acknowledge the help I received in producing this book from my wife Lynelle and our two daughters, Arlene & Cynthia.

They read the original draft then suggested better setting out, wording and spelling to formulate a historical record of my early life and so I wish to publicly thank them for their time and effort.

CONTENTS

INTRODUCTION	7
1. THE UNIQUENESS OF THE RIVERINA	9
2. VIC ROBB BACKGROUND	13
JOHN ROBB - My Great Grandfather 1829-1905	13
ALBERT ROBB- My Grandfather 1881-1936	14
VIC ROBB- My Father 1912-1994	19
3. NELL ROBB BACKGROUND	23
NELL ROBB, MY MOTHER 1918-2016	23
ALBERT BEE, 1877-1939 - MARY JANE BEE, 1884-1963	23
4. WYVERN STATION	27
5. THE FAMILY EXPANDS	29
6. LIFE ON THE STATION	33
7. THE RIVERINA LANDSCAPE	39
8. SWAGMEN	45
9. WORLD WAR II	49
10. NATIVE TREES	53
11. MEMORIES ON THE STATION	57
MEAT PRODUCTION	57
CONTACT WITH INDIGENOUS PEOPLE	57
DROUGHTS AND SAND STORMS	58
12. SOME PERSONAL REMINISCENCES	63
13. WEATHER & SOCIAL EVENTS - WYVERN	67
14. A MOVE TO CALDWELL	73
15. LOCKSLEY	81
16. HOT SUMMERS	85
17. A YOUNGSTER'S OBSERVATIONS	87
18. DROVERS	91
19. RABBITS	95
20. THE SHEEP INDUSTRY	99
21. THE ADVANCE OF AGRICULTURE	103
22. YANCO AGRICULTURAL HIGH SCHOOL	107
23. 1956 FLOOD	117
24. THE OUTCOMES OF THIS PERIOD IN MY LIFE	121

INTRODUCTION

THE RIVERINA has been described as "a vast Old Man and One Tree Plains that became known as the Saltbush Country with the township of Deniliquin designated its capital".[1]

I was born in the Riverina on 29th March 1940 and lived through severe droughts, storms and the occasional flood. The following pages are a glimpse of my personal experiences, first on "Wyvern Station", Bringagee during 1940 to late 1948, then my life mainly at "Locksley", Caldwell, which is west of Deniliquin, from 1949 to 1957.

I begin by creating a summary of the uniqueness of the great Riverina basin, then a glimpse into the lives of my grandparents on both sides and how my parents grew up and met in Griffith. Following that is a broad description of the images planted and painted on my mind as I grew up in that Riverina environment.

Graham Robb, May 2018

---

1. from *Saltbush Country* by John E.J.Bushby, privately published with the assistance of the Library of Australia History 1980.

THE UNIQUENESS OF THE RIVERINA

THE RIVERINA, a rich New South Wales farming region of 9,576,964 hectares, stretches from the Murrumbidgee River to the north and the Murray River to the south and includes a number of smaller rivers and creeks in between.

The Murray runs west until it reaches the town of Echuca. Then it does a long sweep northwest up past Swan Hill to join the Murrumbidgee River, then on to Wentworth, just past Mildura, to meet the Darling River coming from the north. Rivers are the silent life blood of the Riverina and for over one hundred years have been used to irrigate the region, providing vast tracts of farmland with water. Wide open plains, flat plains country that provide shimmering mirages, native trees and plants and varied birdlife all combine to complement this network of rivers and make this country unique and amazing. A great area north of the Edward River is known as the Black Soil Plains and this flat country is mostly covered in saltbush.

All these things combined to leave an indelible impression on my young mind during my growing up years in this diverse region from 1940 to 1956. The phenomenon of mirages in particular hold a special memory for me. They appeared to move forward, either slowly as I rode my bike or more quickly as I sat in a farm station vehicle bouncing across a big paddock. The mirage appears and from a distance it looks like a stretch of water several hundred metres ahead, shallow, and varying in widths yet without a defined edge or border. They generally appear bright and clean yet they hover over the dirty and dusty track or paddock yet never materialise.

I relished the utter silence of the big wide open country as a child, quiet enough to hear an occasional bird calling its mate in the distance. This blanket of silence covered you whether in the open plains, or in a clump of trees, rarely interrupted by a sound of people or a motor vehicle. Just a thick aloneness, providing space to think; or talk to one's self, and not be interrupted by time or responsibility. To watch the eagles and hawks soaring high in the sky on a thermal stream or see a lone Kestrel swooping down hundreds of metres towards a sign of living food, just an innocent mouse or rabbit moving quietly on the ground below. This was the beautiful silence of the vast beauty of the Riverina.

A further permanent memory of this amazing countryside is getting out into nature and experiencing the incredible range of vegetation. To see and touch so many different types of trees, bushes and shrubs, living alone or in clumps, was awe inspiring. To realise each was relying on the particular soil mixture around its root system. Some of these plants flower annually, others just with the right amount of rain or sunshine, different each season. Some are tall and straight, others misshapen and gaunt with arms stretched out in various directions. There are the spritely young trees and the ancient ones, gnarled and broken, yet still showing strong signs of life.

So many different plants flourish in the good seasons and disappear in the times of drought. Often when the rain comes, a myriad of plants, from very small to large, all fight for their development, and some show off a flower that has originally been painted and perfected by their creator God. For some of these plants the season has to be just right for them to germinate, and that may only be every ten or fifteen years. Others are annual or bi-annual. Birds, insects, reptiles and mammals all enjoy their protection or potential as food.

No two seasons are the same, so every year produces differing ground cover. There are generally very cold winters and very hot summers, with beautiful springs and autumns. But some seasons are more hot or cold, dry or wet than others, creating variation in ground temperatures and uncertainty in floral responses. The Riverina is a kaleidoscope of plant life and flowering beauty, as well as many different birds and insects, and each month this changes as climate variations come in to play.

The Riverina is also known as the land of plenty - plenty of heat, plenty of dust and plenty of flies.

There are many books written about this area, its people, the drovers, wagon teams, and general historical events and achievements. We as Robb's have a part in this history, and I believe we should be proud of our heritage.

VIC ROBB BACKGROUND

JOHN ROBB - My Great Grandfather 1829-1905

JOHN ROBB was born in Douglass, Kirkcudbright, Scotland in 1828 and came out to settle in Australia after his young wife died. It was with mixed feelings he left his family and the familiar life he experienced in Scotland. He came out when only 25 to start a new life in a country publicised as a land of opportunity. The buzz word was gold so he moved to a small community called Newstead, near Yandoit in central Victoria. He worked hard as a gold miner and during his time there met a young lady, Mary Morgan. They were married there in the local Presbyterian Church in November 1864. He was 35 years old.

Over the next thirteen years they had six children, although two died in infancy. Because there was no future in trying to find gold they moved further north in 1877 to Echuca, close to the New South Wales border, where three more children were born. Echuca had become renowned for its bustling paddle steamer industry along the Murray River. As they had little assets or cash from the failed gold diggings they moved into a small cottage in Goulburn Road, Echuca. Later the family moved closer to the main harbour to an area known as "Shinbone Alley" Echuca, a row of rough houses just above the Murray River Sawmills near the river. John was an engine mechanic or engine driver and worked on the building of the rail and traffic bridge over the Murray River at Echuca and he also found work on paddle steamers there in Echuca.

While living in Echuca they had their eighth baby on the 29th March 1881 and named him Thomas Albert, followed by a ninth child, a girl, in 1883. They likely missed some schooling and survived on hand-me-downs as older brothers outgrew their clothes. Seven years later, about 1890, John and

Mary decided to move north to the quiet town of Hay. By this time their children numbered only six because two had died in infancy and Andrew had died aged six from drowning, in 1881. They loaded a large wagon and travelled the 200 kilometres to start a new life across the border in this New South Wales town of Hay, in the Riverina. This was a long trip for the family and no doubt tested their resolve to move as each long, jarring and dusty day just followed the one previous.

Leaving the village and hotel at Pretty Pine around 100 kilometres north of Echuca the country became wide open, treeless and flat. They pushed on because of a lack of water and also a lack of natural grass for their horse. There was mainly Saltbush and the horse was not accustomed to such vegetation. The family arrived in Hay with virtually no friends and no work and just the big canvas tent to live under on the bank of the Murrumbidgee River.

There's no record of their family's living conditions over the next few years but it appears that the pressure of life, and possibly the difficulty in finding enough work, impacted on John. Within two or three years he became an alcoholic while living there. Sadly he eventually left his family and went to Castlemaine in Victoria, then later to Deniliquin, New South Wales where he died on 24th November, 1905.

ALBERT ROBB- My Grandfather 1881-1936

THOMAS ALBERT ROBB was known by his second name Albert, and generally this was shortened to Bert. Bert had a hard upbringing, being in a large family without his father John as a breadwinner and this was to affect his whole life.

After his father John left the family in Hay, around 1900, local citizens and shearers organised an appeal and raised money which helped his mother Mary buy a little two-roomed cottage on four acres on the edge of town in Short Street, Hay. How difficult it must have been for the family, with several of the children being late teenagers and young adults by now, living in a two roomed cottage on the outer edge of the town.

There were no other family members living in Hay so Bert was deprived of relatives.

However Bert soon grew up and obtained work as caretaker of Hay cemetery. He met a young lady, Bessie Irvine Newman, in Hay and they were married, when he was 27, on the 12th of October, 1908, in the Parsonage of the Methodist Church, Lachlan Street, Hay, by Rev Herbert Edward Bellhouse. Bessie was born to John Clement & Euphemia McIntosh Newman in Wentworth, in the far south west of New South Wales. It is said her family disowned her for marrying a commoner. The wedding certificate states Bert was a labourer and Bessie was noted as conducting domestic duties. Bert's father, John, had died three years earlier.

Later Bert became a professional fisherman on the Riverina rivers, always on the move to find good water holes.

There were many tributaries feeding into the Darling and Murray Rivers, including the Murrumbidgee, Lachlan and Edward Rivers, the small Wakool River and the Yanco, Colombo and Billabong Creeks. The Darling River and its tributaries can be muddy gutters or roaring dirty rivers depending on the seasonal rains falling into their upper reaches, particularly western Queensland where these rivers flow into the Darling. They wind around the countryside like snakes in the bush.

On each bend the outside of the river is steep and deep and currents cut into the land. The inside is shallow and often sandy due to the current slowing down and eddying and dropping silt. Eventually over time the river cuts through the bends, creating creeks and waterholes known as billabongs. In the drier times water will flow slowly along the bottom of the river, and be quite cool, and the top remains still and warm. The Darling River flows into the Murray River just below the town of Wentworth. The Lachlan River runs into the Murrumbidgee River above the town of Balranald through several channels. It used to stop running on occasions before the Wyangala Dam, above Cowra was completed in 1935.

Bert and other professional fishermen generally fished in a certain pattern. They would camp along the river in a small tent

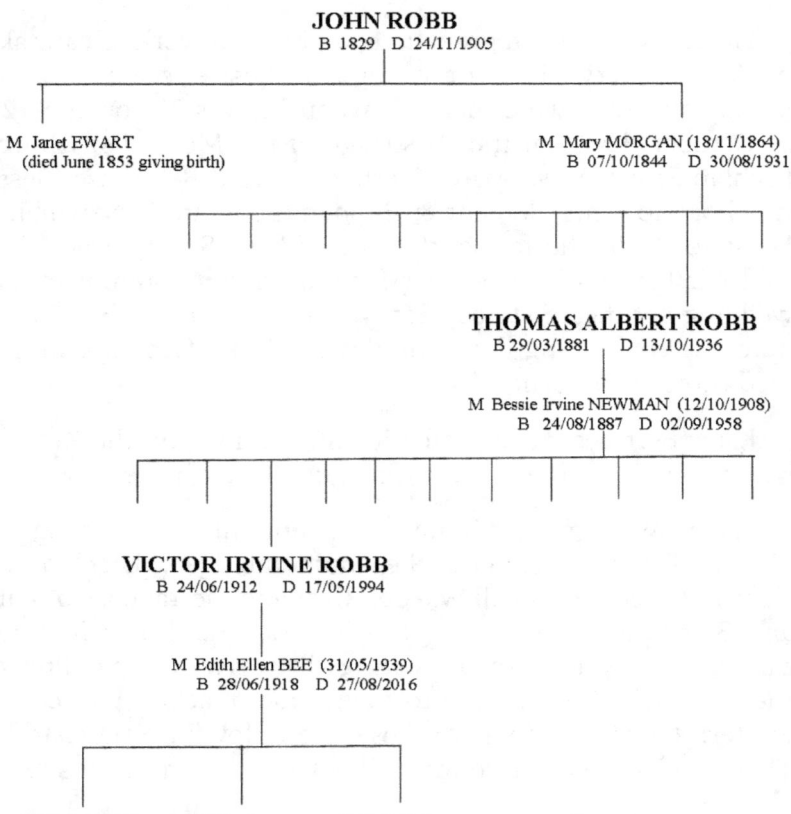

after choosing what they thought was an 'ideal spot' to catch fish. A place with deep water holes and old fallen gum trees fanning out into the water often proved best because fish tend to feed around these trunks and rotting limbs. Some fishermen would have a small one man boat that they pulled on wheels behind their push bikes.

For bait they would dig around the ground at the base of trees looking for specific holes. Using a piece of wire with a twisted screw end on it, the men would insert the wire down the hole, often up to about a metre in depth, turning it around a few times then pulling it up hoping to see a large white grub on it, known as a Bardi Grub. Aboriginal people called these Witchetty grubs and the Murray cod fish loved them when put on a fisherman's line. Other times the fisherman would dig in the mud for worms or pull loose bark from the trees looking for moths and grubs.

In the late spring longicorns beetle larvae could be pulled from holes in the tree trunks under loose bark. These were also pulled out using curled wire and were often 4 to 6 centimetres long and quite fat. Alternative bait was the flesh inside the big river mussels often found in the sandy parts of shallow water.

The fishermen had two ways of catching fish. If they had a little boat they would put in cross lines. A line or heavy string would be taken across the river and tied to a tree root or limb just above the water line on each side of the river. Hanging from this would be a number of short lines with baited hooks down into the water. Next morning it would be pulled up hopefully with several caught fish.

The other way was using lines. They would have a number of these tied to tree roots or pegs on the bank. The baited lines were thrown out and then often hooked over a forked stick a metre or so above the ground and at an angle towards the bank to act as a lever against the pull of the fish. This stops the fish getting tangled in the rubbish in the river. They would often hang a jam tin with a couple of little stones tied in it or a sheep bell on that stick, so that when a fish was hooked the tin would rattle.

To keep their catch of fish fresh they would dig a small hole, line it with a wet hessian, wheat bag or sugar bag around the inside edge and bottom, and put the gutted fish in on layers of fresh gum leaves, periodically wetting the contents. When sending fish to markets for sale, either locally or by train as far away as Sydney, they would pack them similarly in bags or sometimes in wooden kerosene tin crates. Local fishermen were great authorities on the rivers and creeks and the various fish, as well as on the moon and seasons, but perhaps not so good with manual labour or relating to people.

It seems certain that Bert and Bessie and their growing family moved around between Hay and Deniliquin during the years 1909 to 1931 because their children were born at various times in one or other of those towns.

World War I and the Great Depression occurred during this period which caused serious hardship for most families and particularly those in the bush.

I am sure grandad would have become very quiet and depressed when week after week he only caught a few small fish that kept his family fed but made no money from the fish market or even a nearby farmer or passing drover.

About 1930 and in the grip of the Great Depression, Bert and Bessie took the younger members of their family by wagonette up the Darling River from Wentworth to near Bourke, where their last child, Paul, was born, making a total of eleven children. It was during winter so would have been very cold at night and the family were short of food and warm clothes. They lived on a small portion of bread each day and sometimes fish, caught by Bert in a dingy they carried on the wagonette.

Within two or three years of Paul's birth it seems Bessie moved with the younger children to Sydney. In 1936, at the age of 55, Bert became ill in Hay hospital. His son Bern took him by train to Hammondville, near Sydney where his wife was staying with family. He died later that year, on October the 13th.

VIC ROBB- My Father 1912-1994

VICTOR IRVINE ROBB, always known as Vic, was born June 24th, 1912, and was Bert and Bessie's third child. It was a hard upbringing for the children and Vic struggled to improve his life rather than following the examples set by his father and grandfather. When he left school he began working for a newspaper in Hay, and then went fishing for a time with his dad. He spent some time with Perry Bros circus looking after their performing dogs, and this included going with one of his brothers with the circus to Tasmania. His older brother had got work with the circus and arranged for Vic to join the travelling circus. He held this job for some twelve months. Once he started working he regularly sent money to his mother to help her maintain the younger family members.

In 1929 at age 17 he moved north and began work at "Gundabooka Station", located 50 kilometres from Bourke down the Darling River, and stayed there some five years during a big drought. The workers spent many weeks cutting branches off trees to feed the starving sheep. Vic then went further south in 1934 down to "Cowl Cowl Station" between Booligal and Hillston for over four years. Cowl Cowl was a huge station at that time covering 400,000 acres and reaching almost to where Griffith later became a town. The station was renowned for having its own wool scouring machinery. It was recognized as one of the best grazing properties in the area.

Vic then moved even further south to "Wyvern Station" near Bringagee, west of Darlington Point, and began working there on 20th May 1938 in the early stages of what became another prolonged drought.

Vic had been involved at weekends with the Griffith Baptist church and particularly their youth programme. His brother Keith was married and living in Griffith and he had a married sister Elsie living there as well, and they were all involved with the same church. When Vic moved to Wyvern Station he would ride his bike 50 kilometres to Griffith early Saturday morning and sleep the night with his families before riding back Sunday afternoon. He was greatly attracted to young Nell Bee who was involved in the church there and no doubt during the long hours of riding his bike back and forth he may have been thinking about the possibility of marriage and their future together.

Vic built a little house on the station from local timber and used wheat bags sewn together and whitewashed, for walls. The little house had a concrete floor and corrugated iron roof. Another man who lived nearby had done the same thing earlier so he and others helped build the cottage after work and on the weekends. Vic dug steps into the steep river bank so he could bring kerosene buckets full of water up for use in the house.

Vic, then 27, and Edith Ellen (Nell) Bee were married in Griffith on 31st May 1939 with a small wedding party in attendance.

Bringagee Railway Station taken about 1944.

Fabian's Bend on the Murrumbidgee River in Wyvern Station.

NELL ROBB BACKGROUND

NELL ROBB, MY MOTHER, 1918-2016

ALBERT BEE, 1877-1939 - MARY JANE BEE, 1884-1963

IT WAS IN YORK, northern England that Albert Bee, the fourth child to Edward and Mary Ann (nee Rumley) Bee, was born on 29th December, 1877. At age 22 he commenced three years with the British Army during the Boer war, from 1899 to 1902.

When Albert was nearly 25 years old he met Mary Jane North and they were married 16th June 1909. Within three years they took up the challenge to venture out to Australia, the Land of the Southern Cross.

Albert and Mary Bee walked up the gangplank of the TSS (Triple Screw Steamship) "Demosthenes" on the morning of Thursday January 18th 1912. They carefully carried some of their possessions with them up onto the deck, including some special wedding presents. Elsewhere on the ship was a big wooden chest full of possessions and several other wooden and leather cases with all their worldly goods.

After being shown their cabin they returned to the side railing to wave farewell to Albert's parents Edward and Mary Ann Bee and Albert's siblings, Ernest, Tom, Mary, George and Alice. Also there to bid farewell were Mary's parents, James and Sarah Anne North, and Mary's siblings James, Sarah, Susan, Maud, Charles, Lucy, Harriet, William and Elizabeth. There were no doubt very mixed feelings for Albert and Mary as they realised they were leaving their families behind. Would they ever see them again? Would they lose contact with some of their siblings? They were embarking on this journey to Australia through an assisted passage scheme to start a whole new life together.

Perhaps lumps were forming in their throats and tears welling up in their eyes as the realisation of this great break away from home and family began to overwhelm them. Were they doing the right thing? There was no chance of reassessing their dream plans now. The excitement of a new life, of prosperity and a whole new world may have been too much to even think about.

A surviving document, which I have, shows that early in the afternoon a siren blew advising them the ship was about to lift the gang plank and pull up the anchors. They left the port of Gravesend at 3.15 pm, along with a large company of passengers waving frantically as the ship moved out and away. Tomorrow they would pull into Plymouth and more passengers and goods would embark for Australia. The night was probably long and hard for them both. There would have been so many new noises and smells and emotions all mixing together through the hours of darkness.

They departed Plymouth in a "stormy gale with squally high head sea", according to the ships log book. Captain A. Robb advised everyone the ship was new, being only on its second voyage to Australia. She was 11,400 tonnes and the trip would average around 350 miles every 24 hours of travel. The ship's report noted,

"By the time we got out of the Channel a large quantity of the passengers are not feeling as they ought, they refuse the good things placed at their disposal at meal times but by the fourth day out, sea legs are obtained and several energetic members of the passengers form a sports committee and several classes of sports are started, to suit young and old alike, whist drives, dances, concerts etc and it is hardly to be credited the amount of vocalists and instrumentalists there are to be found aboard".

The journey to Australia was going well and I imagine Albert and Mary were enjoying the company and the activities on the steamship. On Tuesday the 30th January they were told they had crossed the equator early that morning. That night no doubt they again experienced feelings of homesickness and loneliness. They possibly would have talked about their home and memories of their growing up in Sheffield Park, a suburb of York. York, at that time was the hub of the railway network and a large confectionery manufacturing centre was established there. It was only a few kilometres north east of Leeds which they visited at times and was originally a walled city at the confluence of the Ouse and Foss Rivers. At the time Albert and Mary left for Australia the city had a population of around 95,000.

They may have reminisced over many friends they had made at school, at church and in the neighbourhood. It is likely that they wondered if they would see many of these people and places again or would it all change before they ever went back? Their conversation may have floated across to the future, discussing questions like, what work they might do? Did they want to live in Sydney or go into the country? What would places look like compared to home? How would they make friends and so many other unknown scenarios were discussed. I wonder how long it was before they eventually retired to bed, and how many mixed emotions they were feeling as they drifted off to sleep to the drumming of the engines under their floor.

Records show that the ship eventually arrived, after negotiating the dangerous rip at Port Phillips Heads, Melbourne on Saturday the 24th of February and a couple of days later went on to Sydney.

Albert's first employment position was working as a greenkeeper at Leura Golf Course in the Blue Mountains west of Sydney. Then he spent four years looking after a property near Braidwood in the far south east of the state. The couple then moved to Manilla near Tamworth where he worked on several farms.

Edith Ellen, my mother, (known as Nell) was Albert & Mary's only child. She was born at Manilla, a few miles north of Tamworth, 28th June 1918.

Young Nell suffered dengue fever, followed by rheumatic fever at the age of nine. Many years later she recalled some painful hospital treatments given to her including the use of towels dipped in boiling water, rung out and wrapped around her knees and elbows. This was done several times a day and caused blisters which the nurses then burst and painted with iodine which stung terribly.

In 1929 when Nell was 11 years old the family moved to Griffith. This was just as the Great Depression began. Every two weeks the unemployed had to register at the local police station. The people who had no work were given vouchers for meat and groceries to certain values depending on the size of the family.

After Nell left school she began working for a dressmaker. Later, in her late teens, she bought the dress-making business. Through all her teenage years she was involved in the Baptist Church at Griffith and helped as a Sunday school teacher and in the Christian Endeavour group, as well as singing in the church. It was through the young people's activities that she met Victor Robb. When she was almost 21 years of age, she then closed the business to marry Vic and moved to live with him on Wyvern Station.

WYVERN STATION

WYVERN STATION was a large sheep station with the southern boundary hugging the Murrumbidgee River. The local main road, only gravel and known as the Murrumbidgee River Road, ran through the station east to west, from Darlington Point to Carrathool. Further north, also east to west through Wyvern Station, ran the main Junee to Hay railway line. Wyvern consisted of 110,000 acres, or 44,000 hectares.

Most of the paddocks were 4 miles (6.5 kilometres) square but a number were subdivided by fences into smaller paddocks. The majority had at least one windmill or bore for drinking water for stock. Each paddock had a name and the majority were named after areas around London, including The Strand, Windsor, Phoenix, Hyde Park, Serpentine, and Chelsea.

The little cottage that Vic had built, and where Vic and Nell were to begin their married life was on the edge of an irrigation paddock. A big diesel pump pulled water from the river into a channel that went some distance before crossing the main road to a large dam. An established woolshed was just north of Bringagee Railway Station on the station's eastern boundary. Some kilometres further north was a station hand's house and then further west a boundary rider's hut.

Vic and Nell's cottage had only very basic furnishings and equipment. There was no bathroom and the weekly bath was taken by putting warm water from an outside copper into a small galvanised round tub on the floor of their small living room.

Just below the cottage was a thickly timbered area stretching several hundred metres to a sweeping bend in the river. This was known as Fabians' Bend and around this sharp bend was a large sand deposit on the inside of the river's curve. On the opposite side was a very steep bank down into deep water.

It was an extremely peaceful area and a great place to gather sticks and wood for the kitchen fire and the outside copper that provided hot water.

Because of its quietness this timbered area was also a great place for lots of different animals including birds, possums, goannas, snakes and insects. In one sense it appeared chaotic, with fallen branches, rotting stumps, misshapen bushes and leaning trees in between clumps of suckers, and tall, majestic, mature red gums. In some places there were patches of grass or a little dry barren area, being a clay pan on which nothing grew. However, often on these dry patches there may be a large active ant's nest. Then there was the odd fallen, decaying tree or large limb pointing up to the sky, but again in no order or common direction. There was always a powerful sense of silence and stillness, except perhaps for the odd squawking of a crow in the distance. Shadows between shards of sparkling light on some fallen leaves created a kaleidoscope of colours. This was nature at its best, a large quiet area of seclusion, with little change over hundreds of years.

So it was on this large sheep station that Nell and Vic began their married life in the little cottage on the bank of the Murrumbidgee River.

How quiet and lonely it must have been for Nell, in those first months, living on Wyvern Station, with the silence of the open country, after having lived and worked in the busy town of Griffith.

Nell's Dad, Albert, died on 3rd November that first year and that was hard for her too, particularly being away from her grieving mother. Leaving her friends, her church responsibilities and the comforts of town life must have been very stressful at times. She began a pioneering life in a bush setting, virtually all alone and with little support other than from her husband. No means of transport into Griffith and no telephone service made it very hard for her to keep regular contact.

In those days married station workers typically received a small wage plus a forequarter of mutton and sometimes vegetables each week as payment.

THE FAMILY EXPANDS

NELL BECAME PREGNANT during that first year on Wyvern Station and in early March the following year, as time for the birth drew near, Vic used a station vehicle to take her into Griffith to stay with her mother.

I was the first child born and was born on 29th of March 1940. Nell had a serious dilemma because I was born with a twisted tube into my stomach, preventing me keeping milk down. Over the first four months of my life I was in hospital and during that time Nell developed breast abscesses. In those days there were no antibiotics. In fact the abscesses had to be lanced without anaesthetic. When she later spoke to her children about this she said how painful it was.

Nell (Mum) remembered that while I was in hospital the staff would talk about a strange figure seen at times on Scenic Hill not far from the hospital. The story was told that an Italian was caught in a storm up on the hill. He set up a camp site in a cave on the hillside. His name was Valerio Ricetti and he lived there for over 20 years from about 1939. He avoided people during the daylight hours and was a recluse but established rock gardens, path ways and walls and was virtually self sufficient. He was a talking point for years and people imagined all sorts of strange stories about him and gossiped about him. In hindsight it is more than likely that he was suffering some kind of mental illness.

Eventually Mum was able to take me home to Wyvern and so began my life in the open plains of the Riverina.

By May of the following year, when I was 14 months old, Mum was driven to Griffith to again stay with her Mum and before long, May 9th, 1942, my sister Audrey Joan was born. She was very healthy and we soon returned to Wyvern, as a growing family.

Later on, on 12th of October, 1944, when I was four and a half and Audrey three, Mum gave birth to their third child, Barbara Gail and our family was complete.

Sadly both of our grandfathers had passed away before we were born. Dad's father (Thomas Albert – Bert) died 13th of October 1936; and Mum's father (Albert) died 3rd of November 1939, just five months before my birth. However as children we were full of life as we grew up in that part of the Riverina.

Living in this quiet area on the riverbank was a great way to start each day. As the sunlight hit the treetops the many different birds began their singing. So many amazing sounds, from the quiet little gossip to loud awakening yells as the different birds began their day of food hunting and territory control. Then as the sun began to actually shine into the trees they resolved to quieten, or scatter, and soon there was a silent blanket across the whole area with just an occasional call from a crow or magpie.

Being right on the river meant there was something different or fresh to see every day. Maybe a floating log slowly moving downstream, or a fish jumping, or a platypus lying on a mud patch. Sometimes a turtle sliding into the water without a ripple or laying still in the water with just its little head pocking above the water. Sometimes we would see an egret strutting along in shallow water or several birds chiacking on some tree limbs. Every day there was something to be enthralled with besides the quietness of the gently moving water.

Probably the most central part of the little family home was the small kitchen table. Mum regularly scrubbed it down with sandsoap to keep it clean and healthy. At this table we ate all our meals, did our correspondence school work, kept warm from the stove in winter and did our chores, like reading or writing. Dad would cut up the meat on it and Mum would use it when making clothes and doing many household chores. Jobs like preparing meals, preparing fruit and jam for preserving, and so many other activities were done on this one kitchen table. When my sisters were babies this table held the little tub as Mum bathed them. It really was the centre of our family life. When it came meal time and the table was set there were special traditional requirements at every meal. Firstly there had to be a table cloth, then butter was placed in a bowl with a flat butter knife in it and jam in a bowl with a special small jam spoon in it.

Like most other households at that time we had a drip safe to keep food cold. A drip safe was a metal structure with mesh sides. The mesh was very fine, too small for flies to get in. On the top was a shallow tray that was filled with water. Hanging down the sides were pieces of hessian or rags. Water slowly syphoned down these rags and dripped into a tray under the body of the structure. The breezes over the wet rags helped keep the safe cool and so the food contents inside were kept somewhat cool. The most common brand of drip safe was a 'Coolgardie Safe'.

LIFE ON THE STATION

AT WYVERN, like all the large stations, there was always work to be done and things unfinished. There were noxious weeds to dig out and destroy or burn. There was always fences to repair or new fences to erect to create smaller paddocks. The windmills had to be checked regularly to ensure that they were working, and worn parts replaced. There were bores and wells to check and sometimes new ones to dig. There was the moving of sheep for shearing, crutching, lamb marking or selling. There was always rabbits to eradicate by trapping, or shooting or by ploughing out their burrows.

House cows had to be milked every day. There were sheep and cattle to slaughter for meat. Besides all this there was irrigation work, storing hay and feed, and the maintenance of vehicles and the farm machinery. In fact there was no end to the work needing to be done. I wonder if, for our father, sometimes it felt like he was in a prison, with no date for release.

The Murrumbidgee River, or called "the Bidgee" by locals, was made a more permanent river supply when the Burrinjuck dam was completed below Yass in 1928. Living on the Murrumbidgee River gave us opportunity to learn about the various fish and animals living in it. Apart from water rats there were Murray cod, redfin, perch, turtles, mussels and Murray crayfish thriving in its waterways. Murray cod with their very large head and weighing up to 75 pounds (34 kilograms) in weight, could live to about 70 years. Our neighbours, the Hills, often went fishing and Dad sometimes set a line to get a fish meal for our family as well. Two other sources of river food to catch were yabbies and crayfish. Yabbies were small crustaceans, like prawns and quite tasty. In many parts of Australia Aboriginals called them Yappees. To catch them we used large tins or one gallon (3.7 litres) fuel drums. We cut the top out of the drum and made a hole near the top and tied a rope through that hole. We then tied a piece of meat in the bottom of it, tossed it out into the water and waited two or three minutes for the drum to sink, then slowly pulled it in. There would generally be some yabbies in it and when we had enough we would take them home, quickly cook them in boiling water, shell and eat them. To catch crayfish we made large drum shaped nets, called drum nets, out of wire netting. Inside we made a funnel of netting from the outer edge almost to the bottom. We then tied a piece of meat or bone in the bottom and threw the net in with a rope attached and next morning pulled it in to capture any caught crayfish. We then cooked them in boiling water and when their shell turned from green to red, they were ready to eat. They had lots of beautiful flesh in their tail and claws, plus a little in their legs and under their back shell. If we found a bunch of their small round pink eggs under their tail we tossed the female back to continue breeding. Crayfish were mostly caught at night and in winter.

Dad had a large, wide wooden boat that he generally tethered to a tree root down the bank. Painted across the rear boards in red letters was the word "Whacko". Whacko was a commonly used word early in the 20th century for being delighted or happy so I suspect that was the feeling for Dad owning his own boat. Dad would sometimes row it out in the river, or across to the other side, to try some fishing. I can remember Dad's youngest brother, Paul, staying with us for a holiday when he was about 16 and I was about five. He spent a lot of the time sitting in the boat dreaming or trying at times to catch fish. I am not sure what happened to the boat when we later left Wyvern but it probably was left upstream with the neighbours, the Hills, on the next farm.

There were occasional times when a trip was made to the small town of Carrathool for shopping. This was only 16 miles (25 kilometres) away. Carrathool is a local aboriginal word for native companion, a large water bird or crane also known as a brolga. We would sometimes see several brolgas together and occasionally they would gracefully dance and do high steps around each other and were beautiful to watch. Originally Carrathool was a busy river port on the Murrumbidgee River but when the rail went through in 1882 the line was moved some five kilometres north of the town and most houses and shops were moved to be near the railway station.

The Murrumbidgee River just metres from our house on Wyvern Station.

An example of a working Lamson Cash Carrier.

On Wade Street, the main street through town, there was a large general store which I recall had huge tubs or actually large wooden boxes with lids, and containers full of grocery items like sugar, tea, flour, salt, potatoes, onions and many other items like stock food and grains.

The staff, all with long white aprons, would measure and weigh these items as ordered and put them in large brown paper bags. This shop also carried many household goods, clothing, kitchenware and sundries. It was quite a busy shop and an eye opening source of intrigue and wonder to us as children.

When a customer bought some goods in this store the sales person wrote out a docket listing the items and their prices. The buyer would give the sales person cash or a cheque and this was folded with the docket and put into a clip under a small round wooden basket above his head. He would then pull a short wooden handle and the basket was propelled, by a strong spring, along a single wire cable to the back of the shop. There a bookkeeper, in an elevated small office or open desk area, would receive the basket, check the docket amounts, often keeping a carbon copy of the docket, and return the original docket, with the correct change, to the sales person.

There were three or four different cable lines across the shop to the cashier so sales people had the basket right at their area of service. This system was known as a Lamson Cash Carrier and to us it was an amazing device that enthralled us as customers came and went. It was quite simple to operate but did look a little cluttered under the shop ceiling with several wires going to different sales points.

West of Carrathool was the larger town of Hay which we went to very occasionally. Hay was known as being very hot and dry; in fact a common reference was made to Hay, (on the Murrumbidgee River), Hell and Booligal (on the Lachlan River). Hay, Hell and Booligal were commonly renowned as being the hottest places ever.

Back at home Dad was often cutting firewood, with an axe, to be used for heating water in the outside copper so Mum could wash the continual supply of soiled baby nappies. The washing was hung on a long wire line between two posts in the ground. The line was held up in the middle by a long forked stick called a prop. Unfortunately on occasions a strong wind would catch the clothes and pull the prop over. The result was either dirty, damp clothes on the ground or a broken prop which Dad then had to replace. Life in our little house was now always busy cooking, feeding and washing.

There was an older Chinese man known as Harry, who was the gardener on the station. His real name was Harry Ah Mow Wong who had made friends with my Dad, Vic. Harry, like many Chinese immigrants, regularly sent most of his wage back home to China. Several years later Harry returned to China and left my Dad and Mum some unusual Chinese memorabilia.

THE RIVERINA LANDSCAPE

LIFE ON THE RIVERINA stations in the first 50 years of the twentieth century was very hard. A number of the wider Robb family, some of our uncles and aunts, lived in and around the Riverina during this period, namely Bourke to the north, Deniliquin to the south, Griffith in the centre, and many places in between.

Some lived on big sheep stations. Working long hours in harsh conditions, they experienced droughts and flooding rains. The owners, managers and staff of these stations operated under a social class system where owners and managers were considered above the other workers and were always referred to as Mr or Mrs, rather than by their Christian names. The workers (labourers) were mostly single men who lived in the supplied staff huts, tents and rooms, near the homestead. There were also gardeners, cooks, maids and general rouseabouts, (unskilled farm labour). The staff were paid a small wage, plus they were generally provided with meals and accommodation.

Vic, like many of these farm workers, had to maintain windmills that supplied water either through a well dug by hand into the underground water supply or through bores that went many metres down. At that time there were two popular windmill brands, the Comet and the Southern Cross. The Comet was founded by Sidney Williams in Rockhampton, Queensland in 1879 and was later manufactured in Dulwich Hill in Sydney. It was known as 'The Rolls Royce" of windmills and in 1920 the federal government introduced contracts using the Comet windmills for all railway stations, schools, government buildings and stock routes throughout Australia. The Southern Cross brand was started by the inventor George Griffiths and the Griffiths Brothers began production in 1903 at Toowoomba Foundry Pty Ltd. There was some rivalry between station owners as to which windmill was the better and Dad often referred to this when we lived at Caldwell.

Dad also had to do fencing, rabbit and burr (noxious weed) eradication, land clearing, and all facets of sheep work including mustering, lamb marking, crutching, yarding for drafting off market lambs, and generally helping at shearing time. Once the shearing was completed several men and sometimes Dad would help roll the bales of wool that were stored in the shearing shed to the loading deck outside the shed. Then he would help load them onto big horse drawn wagons to be taken to the rail centre in Hay. There was always work to do and a varied number of tasks to complete.

Up until the 1940's carriers using wagons drawn by bullocks or draught horses carted the bales of wool or bags of wheat to railway stations or to loading points on the rivers. There paddle steamers would take the produce to large towns like Echuca, Hay, Wentworth and Mildura. When the carting was finished many of these teams went onto sheep stations using their bullocks and horses to dig dams for water. They alternatively were employed to clean out previously sunken dams. Some of these dams were easy to clean and remove dried mud but others were difficult because soft sand had settled in the bottom and this was hard to remove and was heavy and slippery in the scoops they used. Generally these team animals were very reliable and were treated kindly and with respect and care by their owners.

Most of the Riverina, except the Murrumbidgee Irrigation Area (MIA) around Griffith, is a black soil plain. Vast areas, particularly around Hay are very flat and nearly tree-less. When it rained the black soil became soft mud and many wagons, vehicles and livestock became bogged in it. Many roads in those days were only unsealed tracks, particularly on the stations, and they often went through swamps and over small hills requiring extra care by drivers and carriers to avoid tipping a wagon or vehicle over.

The Riverina became the base for the Australian wool industry and many station owners made a lot of money, employed lots of people and were at the forefront of new farming methods.

Across the Riverina there were many kangaroos and emus and we often saw them as we moved through paddocks. The two common kangaroo species in the Riverina are the eastern grey and the red kangaroo. A nineteenth century Englishman declared that kangaroos have a most efficient means of locomotion and stated that their efficiency derives from the geometry of their legs and the elasticity of their tendons: the faster the animal hops, the harder it lands; the harder it lands, the more energy is stored and released in the next hop.[2]

Young joeys look out from their mother's pouch or hide completely inside. We often saw that if the mother was suddenly frightened while grazing, the joey would dive head first into the pouch and as the mother bounded away, two grey legs remained poking out. If we went towards a number of kangaroos grazing the older kangaroos would stand up tall watching. They held their upper paws crossed on their middle, standing still and erect, waiting until the last moment to turn and bound away, their big tail pounding the ground as they went.

On the open plains country like Wyvern Station there were also many emus. We would sometimes see their nest with up to 20 eggs in them. They were just a basic hollow on the ground. They have an eight week incubation period. Their eggs have several shades of colour from dark blackish green to off white. The shells have several layers of colour and aboriginals and white men carefully peel off the layers with a sharp knife to produce beautiful carvings and scenes.

Later we were shown some of these by part aboriginals who came to shear the sheep at "Locksley" near Caldwell when we lived there.

Amazingly the male emu stays on the nest then remains with the young until they are nearly fully grown. The female does not

---

2) From *The Bush* by Don Watson, p.373. First published by Penguin Group (Australia) 2014.

stay with the male all this time but when the young go out on their own the pair will rejoin and stay together until the next hatching season.

We would watch them when they were quietly feeding. They were very sedate and strutted along majestically, then would quickly reach down to pick up seeds on the ground. Emu oil was used extensively by aboriginals for bruises and strains, according to several historians. Emus like eating Quondong, that is, the seeds on Quondong trees. They swallow the red flesh covered seed and leave the hard central stone in another area, when they pass their droppings. The hard wrinkled seeds or nuts have a medicinal oil and fat in them, and often are used as marbles in Chinese Checker boards.

I understood that kangaroos and emus are unique in that they cannot walk, hop or move backwards.

Another special feature of the Riverina is its many grasses and plants. The soil type has a big impact on the type of plant grown. In a space of 100 metres there can be differences such as clay to sand, rich to poor in nutrients, soft to hard ground. Different grasses, trees, and vegetation live in these varied soil patch areas. This is seen more clearly near and away from river banks, as one walks up a hill or crosses a flat dry swamp area. Each paddock has areas of varied and changing soil types.

Drovers in the early days noticed this as they followed slowly behind their grazing stock. George Seddon, an environmentalist scientist and writer noted that "Plants are ranked as weeds if they are contrary to human intentions".[3] Farmers over time have removed, burned and poisoned plants they believed to be "weeds" and in many places this has caused soil erosion and the land has become hard and lifeless. As a result rain runs off the higher points and does not soak in to allow the soil to hold moisture for tree roots and the subsoil, causing long term environmental damage.

---

3. The Old Country: Australian Landscapes, Plants & People, p.219, Cambridge University Press, 2005.

One of the real problems facing people living in the Riverina was the frustration of flies, which were particularly bad in summer when people were more likely to be outside their homes. The flies were attracted to human body smells and moisture. Dozens of them would swarm onto people's sweaty backs, and any excess movement caused them to rise en masse, and then quickly resettle on shirts or blouses. Flies would get in our eyes and ears and sometimes, when talking or eating, even into our mouths, occasionally to be swallowed. They would wait, ready to fly inside when any door was opened. The act of waving away the persistent swarms of flies led to the term, the Australian wave. These insects were the small bush flies. Sometimes they were in plague proportion and drove sheep, horses, dogs and even people mad. When walking in the grass we would often see bush flies swarming on fresh warm cow pads or animal faeces where they laid their eggs in the warmth.

Then there were also the blow flies, a larger more annoying and destructive variety. These flies breed in warm living places on freshly deceased animal carcasses. They would lay eggs on sheep around their anus (known as crutches) where faeces catch in the wool and soon maggots appeared and would burrow into the skin and cause pain and distress to the sheep. They would also do the same when sheep got foot rot in wet times and the maggots got under the sides of their hooves. I have described this more in the later chapter concerning sheep.

Ants were also a real problem and we had to be careful not to encourage their presence or have places where they could nest and breed. There were bull ants, meat ants, green head ants, white ants and tiny ants that got into everything. Most of these varieties had stings too. We had to put empty fruit tins full of water under the legs of the drip safe and meat safes. Ants would not climb over the water to climb up the legs.

When walking through timbered areas, particularly around Fabien's Bend, we had to watch in the warmer months for both black and brown snakes, and for big goannas that would scurry up a tree near us. It was a known fact that snakes or goannas when disturbed could run at people rather than escape to a hollow log or tree. The goannas were large grey varieties that could stand high on their rear legs to check out intruders and run extremely fast on their big legs. They have a bottom jaw that can hinge, like some snakes, to open much wider and so they can consume largish animals, rabbits or birds without chewing them.

SWAGMEN

DURING THE GREAT Depression in Australia (1929-32), Australia's unemployment rate rose to just over 30% in 1932, although it was higher in the bush. Many men wandered (tramped) the outback looking for work to support their families back home. Many were business people, others not so educated, but all desperate for money to survive. They would call into station homesteads for work and food and often were chased off with some bread, tea leaves or sugar or if they were lucky a piece of meat as well. Many were unkempt, disillusioned and in poor health. These men were commonly referred to as Swagmen as they carried their belongings with them in a bedroll or swag.

Occasionally a swagman would appear at our house. They either saw our little house in the distance when walking along the main road, or saw it when they called at Wyvern Station homestead. Either way they hoped to get some food, and maybe somewhere to wash and sleep for a night or two. As young children we were always a bit afraid of them coming around our place, they seemed to us as strange intruders into our sheltered world. Dad would offer a meal of meat and some tea leaves but we didn't have much so we were limited in the help we could provide them. There was a saying that a swagman had so little tea leaves that when he made a drink, the tea came out of the billy on crutches. It was a way that I got to learn about them and feel sorry for them.

Swagmen never travelled on a horse because a horse always required regular food and water; whereas swagmen had the freedom to stop anywhere; where there was a log or some trees, a dry creek, or a fence to climb through to reach a dam or waterway. In fact if they were near a station homestead and it didn't look to be a good place to approach for sustenance they could lie down and hide behind a big log. If riding a horse they

Our family outside our home in about 1946 and 1947.

would easily be seen and generally asked to move on. Even if their boots were well worn and tied up with a piece of wire or string they still walked. They were often called sundowners or whalers and if in the Riverina, Murrumbidgee whalers. They were well experienced in getting food at a station homestead. They aimed to arrive at the front door just before dusk, knowing the owner would not get them cutting wood or doing gardening to earn their tucker or dinner because it was almost dark.

There were some swagmen who would carry seeds in a matchbox and if the property owner told him to get off his property he would pull out the matchbox and show the seeds and the farmer, thinking they might be noxious weed seeds would condescend and give him food. These swagmen were colloquially known as "Bryant and May swagmen", after the matchbox company Bryant and May whose familiar logo was on the matchbox they carried. This concept was also called the Bryant and May scheme or trick.

Compared to a drover, who would eventually return home to his wife, his family, or his mates, a swagman had no end in sight; not any return address, or base to go back to. Banjo Patterson's ballad said,

"Clancy's gone to Queensland droving and we don't know where he are".[4]

Sending him a letter may have found him, but not if he were a swagman. Banjo Patterson also wrote Waltzing Matilda in 1895 near Winton which tells a story of a jolly swagman. Was he jolly by nature, or was he fat, or was he described this way because he was a jolly nuisance? He would not be fat or oversize if he was a swagman as they often didn't eat very well. They saw more dinner times than dinners.

Today we might say they were physically challenged or damaged, and no doubt many were suffering mental illness and may have come from broken homes and lived through abusive upbringings. They may have had other physical shortcomings.

---

4. *Clancy of the Overflow*, first published in the Bulletin Magazine, 21st December 1889 as written by A.B. Banjo Patterson.

Some were well educated but suffered a mental breakdown, or had serious disenchantment with society, or government, or a myriad of other problems or struggles that made them feel a failure. They knew poverty, loneliness, terror and hunger and they did not trust people who were richer or more educated than themselves. Often they were referred to as "a few bob short of a full quid", a bob being a shilling and a quid being a pound in those days. Other people said that money talks but to swagmen their money only said good bye.

Swagmen travelled light, generally with a blanket rolled up on their back, which was referred to as their swag. Inside the blanket would be a few possessions like shaving equipment, a few pieces of cutlery; and sometimes a spare shirt and trousers. This concept was the basis for the term used on them of "Humping their Bluey", a common light-coloured blanket that they used to wrap their possessions in. On their belt would be a mug, a billy can and often some string. They may carry tobacco, odd pieces of food and a few sundries. On their head would be a hat, often with a net over it or several pieces of corks hanging by string around the brim to disturb annoying flies.

Not many swagmen actually came to our house on Wyvern but they were often spoken about and we were intimidated if one did appear.

WORLD WAR II

DURING THE SECOND World War there were a number of Japanese prisoners housed outside Hay in camps. On 27 June 1945 some of these prisoners escaped. Over that day and the next we saw small aeroplanes flying low as they followed the main road a kilometre or less north of us. At first we didn't know why the planes were flying and why so low but the next day we were told they were hoping to find some of the escaped prisoners. This was all very scary for us not knowing if these prisoners might turn up demanding food or protection or even attack us. None were found around Wyvern Station fortunately.

Petrol rationing began in October 1940 and private cars were only allowed enough to travel about 25 kilometres each week. There was not enough petrol for out of town people during the war and many station vehicles were fitted with charcoal burning units to provide fuel. The engines would be started with power kerosene and when they got hot they would be switched over to gas from the charcoal burner. A charcoal burner burns the gases produced by heated wood and there is the need of some form of fire to heat the wood. The burning charcoal provides heat to burn the wood that produces gas to fire the carburettor. The charcoal burner had to be lit up some time before the vehicle was to be used so that there was gas ready. Petrol rationing didn't cease until February 1950.

During the Second World War the government paid men to burn timber for charcoal. Men burnt logs and timber on the riverbanks across the state in large furnaces, or kilns, the aim being to carbonise the wood before it became ash. Timber was piled up in a cone shape, and then covered with layers of grass and soil. The fire was lit in the centre and the colour of the smoke indicated how it was smouldering and carbonising. This process generally took six to eight days then the pile was pulled apart to cool, then the charcoal was put into hessian bags for sale. Occasionally workers died from carbon monoxide poisoning while dismantling the kilns. The charcoal came in these bags and the men using the vehicles on the stations were covered in black dust. There was a small group on the river up above Wyvern Station who did this as a job.

Food and clothing were rationed during the war as well, which directly affected us. Every man, woman and child was issued with a book of coupons every twelve months. These were normally collected at the local police station. However on the sheep stations there was generally a man who acted as the station office administrator. He paid the employees, kept records of stock movement, all purchases and sales, weather conditions and rainfall and generally recorded all manner of station activities.

This role on Wyvern Station was undertaken by an Edward C. Newell who was registered to hand out ration coupons during and after the war. He was responsible for completing this for each employee entitled to ration books and cards on Wyvern Station. Rationing regulations were gazetted on 14th May 1942 and were brought in to manage shortages and control consumption. To be entitled to rations, required an identity card and my parents received their first on the 2nd April 1942 from a distribution centre in Junee. Clothing ration cards were issued to them on 3rd June 1944. Each adult was allowed 112 coupons per year. A family had 39 butter coupons, 26 sugar coupons, 104 meat coupons, and 52 tea coupons. There were clothing coupons as well totalling 56 per person.

In December 1946 ration books of cards were replaced by just ration cards but at the same value. It was a great relief for Dad and Mum to get these cards and they were proud to be allocated them, not that they managed to go into a town very often to use them. Every single item was worth so many coupons, so everyone had to carefully work out what to buy and if it really was necessary at that time. Those who didn't smoke cigarettes or pipe tobacco gave their coupons to those who did. Clothes had to be patched and mended and often second hand calico bags were made into clothes or used as patches. Soap was home made from fat from around sheep kidneys rendered down with resin and caustic soda and a little borax. Thankfully for my family most rationing stopped by 1948 when I was eight years old.

Another facet of the war involved civilians who were asked to make camouflage nets for the army. Dad and Mum received big hanks of khaki coloured twine and a special large square of wood to make the mesh the right size. As they were being made the nets were hung on long sticks between trees. Each mesh had to be 8cm across and it took practise to get the knots tight and the meshes square. We used to watch Dad and Mum making them when they had spare time. I believe when several nets were completed they were taken to the homestead and later taken to Bringagee railway station for delivery to Sydney. I was too small to remember how many Mum and Dad would have made but probably only a dozen or so as it was a fairly time consuming work.

The cook on Wyvern, the old Chinaman, Harry Mow would sometimes give Dad little bags of rice during and after the war. He apparently was given supplies and didn't use them. The problem was the bags had lots of weevils in them and my sister Audrey and I used to spread the rice on trays in the sun, and then using tweezers pick the weevils out so our family could have the luxury of eating rice. A tedious job but we had to do it.

NATIVE TREES

THE RIVERINA HAS a significant number of tree species and Wyvern Station grew many of them. Trees are homes to possums, bats, parrots, and owls plus resting places and nesting places for many varieties of birds and insects.

Much of Australia is home to the eucalyptus trees. There are over 850 species of eucalypts and most of them are found only in Australia. They are known generally as gums because they leak out gum or sap when cut or the bark is broken. The sap generally has an oily smell that exudes when a shower of rain hits them. Most of the eucalyptus family have flowers, but their special feature is their leaf. Their leaves have an oily base which causes them to burn easily and crackle as they curl up in the heat.

There are many uses for the eucalyptus oil that can be extracted from these trees. The leaves of eucalypts are hard and not easily digested by animals, except the koala. They contain compounds that make them rough and slow to decompose on the ground. In most eucalypts the leaves hang down to deflect the rain drops and to avoid long spells in the direct sun. They are generally a grey green colour and often long and thin, although some are more round in shape. I remember becoming frustrated when trying to sweep them off our veranda or path, because they were so flat they would stick to the surface or sometimes fly up and land a couple of centimetres away. In the distance they can look bluish rather than green which gives an eerie appearance to the distant landscape.

The river red gums live for hundreds of years and display the effects of living through many droughts and floods. Their great trunks are gnarled and bereft of limbs but higher up they are arms of graceful character and strength that reach out in all directions.

They are silent giants by the waterways and creek beds. Many alive today were living before white man ever travelled across the Riverina. The early settlers cut them down and used the timber for railway sleepers, as well as wharves, housing, fence posts, furniture and to power the paddle steamer engines. There were many millions of trees cut down across Eastern Australia for these reasons. Some giant ones were used as temporary housing for new settlers and aboriginals cut canoes from their sides.

They are well known for their tendency to drop large limbs suddenly and without warning even when there is no wind or even a breeze. Solid branches fall into waterways to become breeding grounds for fish, crayfish and water rats. Man came along and pulled out some of these logs and limbs to make easier travel for the paddle steamers towing large heavy barges loaded with wool, timber or produce. Then man built dams and weirs that changed the natural flow and altered fish stock numbers and even caused rising water tables and salinity, as well as silting and diversion of flow direction. Even to this day these dams and weirs cause faster flows over the spillways which in turn scour the river banks and the moving silt builds up in the river beds. This in turn creates shallower waterways which results in higher flood levels.

Water is deeper in flood times, stays longer and causes more damage to the natural environment. The outside of the bends in the rivers wash out and then the deposited silt and sand builds up on the inside of the curve. The faster flows caused by dams also undermines the great red gum trees and they fall into the rivers and waterways causing havoc for fishermen, boats and swimmers.

In the post World War II era governments established new laws preventing the cutting down, ring barking or destruction of young trees within 20 metres of the riverbank or in watercourse beds and lagoons. This has slowly increased the red gum tree population in the Riverina and Murray Darling system. In fact these are often the only trees seen as one travels the roads and highways and they clearly define waterways across the landscape.

There are also weeping willow trees that people planted along irrigation channels after the Second World War. These are a strong green colour with branches that flow down to the ground, very picturesque but of no value as stock feed or for their timber.

The peppercorn tree is another species in the Riverina region. They have a strong smell and small berries that smell and taste like pepper. Again of little value, except as shade trees for sheep in the summer.

Another tree type is the Murray pine whose timber was used for fence posts or stumps and lining the internal walls of sheds and houses. This was popular because this timber was white ant or termite resistant. The Murray pine timber burns easily and gives off a very pleasant smell when cut or burnt.

Other local trees are silky oaks, pines, mulga, wattle, grey box, boree and various eucalyptus varieties.

In the earlier days of men carving out their own piece of Australia, their paradise in the bush, they spent themselves getting ready to produce food. They cut, grubbed and burned the trees as though those trees were man's greatest pest. The early selectors lived in a world of fire, smoke and ash. The sound of axes hitting trees or trees crashing down when cut was to them victory and power and achievement.

Trees can often live on in our memory, perhaps significant because they grew near where we lived as a child. A tree we often climbed, or perhaps one we planted, or remember because it was small, or the wind whistled in its leaves, or because of its shape, gracefulness, character or special branches, left an image planted in our mind. For example I have a memory of a big log that was shaped like an arch just down from our house. As children we spent lots of time climbing or sitting on it and we referred to it as our big log. Unfortunately it was later badly damaged by tree branches falling on it in a huge storm.

Men have planted avenues of trees in some towns to remember the war dead. Others have written about them like the swagman sitting under the coolabah tree. Trees remind us of freedom, silent power, nature, mystery or tenacity.

Because there are very few areas of stone in the whole Riverina, generations of settlers, miners and farmers used timber for many things. For example, their homes, sheds, furniture, fences and stock holding yards were all made from timber. Many of those early pioneers were also experts in the various types of timbers available and could choose the best for each situation, which is why even today there are original buildings, posts and post and rail fences still in use.

MEMORIES ON THE STATION

MEAT PRODUCTION

CATTLE OR SEVERAL sheep were slaughtered once a week for meat for the manager and staff. They were killed by cutting their throat then the skin pulled and punched off the warm carcass. The beast was then hauled up by a rope through a cross bar between their legs and raised above the ground on gallows, head down. Heavy cattle were generally pulled up on a pivoted timber and the end hooked under a lever to hold it steady. The animal was then gutted, covered with a large hessian bag and wheeled in a barrow into a room enclosed with mosquito or fly wire and left there overnight to dry out before being cut up on a big chopping block.

CONTACT WITH INDIGENOUS PEOPLE

I remember on one occasion going on a special outing. On Saturday 25 November, 1944, Mum, Dad and the three of us children went to Darlington Point to the reopening of the newly modernised little Aboriginal Inland Mission Church. Several years earlier a hunch back disabled aboriginal had been pastor of the little church and had been part of a spiritual revival amongst the aboriginal population there. His name was Bobbie Peters and he had helped organise the erection of a simple church building in 1937. The bag walls soon deteriorated and in 1944 the building was renovated over a nine month period with voluntary labour. We attended the opening and Dad took part in the service by reading Psalm 100. This was the first time I had had any contact with Aboriginal people so it was all a little frightening seeing their culture and mannerisms.

DROUGHTS AND SAND STORMS

In the year of 1944 and through the summer of 1945 there was a terrible drought across much of western NSW, South Australia and Victoria. I was four then and because of the drought the Murrumbidgee River actually stopped flowing. In fact one could walk across it in many places and by dodging water holes not get wet.

In early 1945, for at least a couple of weeks each afternoon huge clouds of dust enveloped everything. It would blow in from the west or the northwest in thick rolling clouds. Lamps were lit because it became so dull and dark inside the house. Because of the drought there was very little feed for the sheep on Wyvern and train trucks loaded with potatoes, onions and pumpkins and bags of stock pellets were left at Bringagee Rail Station on the edge of the property boundary. My dad, Vic, and other boundary riders and workmen carted this food to various paddocks to feed the starving sheep. In some paddocks there were areas of old man saltbush, a salty tasting bush that can grow to two metres high. It is roughly textured, a woody type of plant that is very hardy and generally fairly drought resistant. Sheep eat it when there is nothing else to eat, as they did at that time.

Then one late morning a huge dark, rolling, storm cloud of thick dust crossed the station. To me it looked like a very bad thunder storm approaching but it was unusual in that it was mid morning not like normal storms that mostly came in the late afternoon. The dust was so thick there on Wyvern Station that it filled the water troughs with sand and the men had to clean them out next day to get water in for the sheep. Our little home was filled inside with layers of dust. In fact Barbara was a baby in a cot at the time and there was just a white patch on the sheet under her when she was lifted up. The rest of the sheet and pillow was covered in thick red dust in a matter of an hour or so. The dust storm continued for several days and dust actually blew across the state, over Sydney and on to New Zealand. It was so thick workers got lost in it and had to keep moving until they came to a fence to find their way home. The wind blew roly polys and rubbish against fences and the rolling sand buried fences in some places. Sheep lay down and the sand was so heavy in their wool that many could not get up and they perished. For days the men worked saving downed sheep, trying to clean out water troughs, recover buried fences and find food for the thousands of effected sheep. It was estimated 10 million sheep died from the drought in NSW alone in 1945, and across Australia the loss was around 30 million.

Afterwards there was the cleaning up in our little house. Dusting down every item inside and wiping down shelves and crannies. Brushing and sweeping shovelfuls of dust and leaves. The chimney above the wood stove let in dust and leaves and that brought down soot. It was a big task for Mum and Dad and for weeks after, little patches of dust appeared in many places, including in our clothes stored in boxes.

Fortunately good drought-breaking rains began mid 1945.

One time during 1945 our family were returning to Wyvern Station after spending time in Griffith. Dad was driving the station truck, an ex world war two Chevrolet. He hit a large pothole and the passenger door flew open and Mum fell out. We were scared and frightened as Dad pulled the truck up. He jumped out and ran back. Fortunately we were not going very fast on the rough track and Mum was uninjured, however her handbag flew out and we had to gather some papers the wind was blowing around. Audrey was seated next to Mum and she held onto baby Barbara so no other person was hurt either. That was a very traumatic incident for us all and we thanked God for His protecting hand. There would not have been anyone to help for many kilometres around, had it have been a serious accident, and certainly no telephone service or ambulance should she have needed medical assistance.

Living away out in isolation like we were on that big sheep station meant Mum and us children seldom saw anyone. It was different for Dad because of his work. On occasions we would walk up river as a family, about a kilometre or more, to a family on the next property. There were three adult brothers and an adult sister, Norman, Ted, Harold and Maudie Hill. The farm was in their late parent's name. Ted was often away working his own farm. Norman also worked his own farm below Wyvern where he grew grain and had three draught horses, named Mick, Kate and Rastas, that pulled his machinery and harvester.

Harold unfortunately suffered from Down syndrome. His body was overweight and he would swing his arms out, particularly above his head; and spread his fingers wide. He could barely speak apart from grunts and smiles. He had a passion for boxing and would listen to any fight broadcasts on the radio and people would give him pictures and stories of boxers. He just lived for boxing stories and pictures. He had a particularly large photo of his idol, the famous American Rocky Graziano.

As children we liked him because he was in many ways childlike but we were also afraid of his big body. Maudie was a lovely caring "mother" to him and loved having our family visit. Sometimes we would have supper with her and the special treat for us children was watching her make toast, on a long metal fork on the open fire, which she then gave to us with vegemite on it. We also loved the hot cocoa she made for us. Maudie was not always up at this farm house because she actually owned a house in Narrandera and she and Harold lived there. They came down when things were busy on the farm, such as grain planting or harvest time.

Dad used to have a little Sunday school on Sundays for us three children. He would give each of us a penny for an offering that went into a special tin and would be given periodically to a mission or mission representative. Once or twice a year the Baptist minister in Griffith would come out to our house and spend the day with us. I remember when I was six he asked me to say each letter of the words Holbrook's Worcestershire Sauce on the sauce bottle and as a reward gave me a penny. About once a year we had a visit from a representative of the Bush Church Aid Society, or Bush Mission Society or someone from the Bible Society. They were generally in a wagonette but sometimes in a motorised van with Christian literature on board. There were texts and the name of the ministry painted all along the vehicle. We had little money to buy anything but still appreciated their visit and sometimes they stayed overnight, either near our house in their wagonette or down near the secluded river bend.

We also occasionally had a visit from a hawker. They were single men, generally Indian or Afghan and travelled in wagonettes or occasionally in big motorised vans. There was a bed up the centre and the sides pulled out to reveal all sorts of goods to purchase. There would be kitchenware, clothes and material, sewing goods, water bags, tools and sundry household items for sale. We loved it when they came because we could see all their stock and hear their accent as they talked. Again, not having much spare money to buy anything made it hard but it was very exciting having them at our little house. Mum always seemed able to buy something new and special.

Sometimes we would drive up to Narrandera to see Maudie and Harold in the home she had there, and to do some shopping. The town of Narrandera has a clear dip in the road after crossing the Murrumbidgee River and it rises to the north where the train line runs. It has a big lake, Lake Talbot, which is a popular swimming area. There was also an amazing park area we would visit. It had the usual swings, see-saw, slippery dip and merry go round but also large enclosures of birds, ducks and peacocks wandering around in the open. We would spend what seemed like ages enjoying the nature exhibits, talking to the birds and revelling in the green grass and manicured lawn areas.

SOME PERSONAL REMINISCENCES

THERE WERE STRESSFUL relationship problems in our family at times and this was partly because of the isolation and also because of Dad's hard upbringing, much of that being without a father figure. He could get quite angry when one of us did wrong. He had a wide trouser belt and he would belt us all around the body with it, not just one or two strikes but a number.

They were often for misdemeanors which were not serious and one instance I clearly remember when I was six. Near our house was a large machinery shed and in it was a hay baling machine. We were told not to touch the machine because we may get hurt. My sister Audrey and I went in one day and I turned a large pulley wheel around. I caught my fingers in the cogs of the wheel. Audrey pulled the wheel back and released my fingers but they were bruised and had a little broken skin. When we got home and Dad found what we had done he gave me a severe belting before finding out if any fingers were broken or seriously hurt.

Action before investigation, and I have never forgotten that treatment. I guess I did disobey but the quick punishment could have been more carefully considered in my opinion. Another incidence I remember was when Mum used a cracked dinner plate and he threw the plate and food it held onto the concrete floor and it smashed everywhere. Mum had to clean it up. He really did not give me clear guidance as a role model so I had to learn from others as I grew up.

Mum seemed to me to be very quiet and not involved in Dad's forms of punishment or control. Whether this was because she was afraid of his authority or because her upbringing was in a similar vein, as was so often the case in many families in those times, I am not sure. I certainly never felt personal love or attention from her or felt any touching, hugs or words of encouragement from her. It may have been my fault that I was not a communicator or perhaps I didn't read into their actions and their endeavours to love and help me grow, I don't know. Mum was certainly a good housekeeper and cook but not an outgoing people person, as far as I experienced anyway.

We hardly had any toys or books and used pieces of wood and sticks as play things. We never saw magazines or newspapers so had very little to read. The few books we did have we read and re-read and we knew every detail in any pictures in them. Not having other children to play with meant we never craved for the latest toys or play things, like other children had, because these were unknown things to us. Not mixing with other children made us very shy and really scared when we did happen to meet another family, such as occasionally when we visited our cousins in Griffith.

I remember one time walking up the river a hundred metres or so with Dad while he started up the big diesel irrigation pump. Being an explorer at that young age, and not remembering Dad's instruction, I climbed around the pipe then went to get over another pipe. It was the hot exhaust pipe and I burned a huge patch on my shin. This was another time Dad yelled and hit me without first checking if I was badly burned or even sorry for not heeding his instruction.

In 1947 (25th September) the three of us children (aged 7, 6 & 3) had our tonsils out the same morning in Griffith hospital. I can remember the fear of going into hospital, then the agony for a couple of days after the operation. I don't know why we all had them out but it seemed in those days doctors liked to remove "unnecessary tonsils" early. We all cried most of that afternoon from the pain, blood, and uncertainty of the future. I bled a lot and had to stay in hospital overnight. We remained then in Griffith at our grandmother's (Mum's mother) place for a couple of weeks, living on custard, jelly and mashed potato for the first few days. We found the days rather boring and just swallowing food for the first few days was a terrible experience because we felt hungry and wanted to eat, but it hurt so much.

Thinking of foods I enjoyed as a child, toast with dripping seasoned with salt and pepper was a special favourite. Dripping was liquefied fat that came out of the meat when roasted. It was poured into a china bowl, jug or glass dish and the fat solidified as it cooled down. Below it when it firmed was a dark flavoursome liquid. This juice was generally added when making gravy. Another common addition to bread, toast or scones was treacle, or golden syrup, commonly referred to as Cockies Delight.

Locksley homestead from the front

Caldwell General Store in 1949

WEATHER & SOCIAL EVENTS – WYVERN

ON THE 16TH of November 1946 a storm had been brewing for some time and seemed to be following along the river from the west. As it reached our area it suddenly seemed to increase in its velocity. It was late afternoon and Dad was home so it must have been a weekend. We could hear the roar of the wind outside our house and every few moments a crash of thunder and flash of lightning. Squally gushes of rain beat down on our iron roof. We all stood together in a huddle between the living area and bedroom area, peering out a window to the north. The group of peppercorn trees a little way over were bending and swaying and every couple of minutes a small branch on one would break away from the strain of the wind.

I remember the five of us huddled in the little passageway hearing the roar of the wind and noises like crashing trees and all of us were too frightened to speak. It was a terrifying few minutes and even Dad and Mum were silent and fearful as to what might happen to our little home. Then quite suddenly the wind died down and the rain faded away to a sprinkle. We were just so relieved our little house survived the mini tornado.

Soon we all went outside to see what damage may have been done from the ferocious wind. We were all dumbfounded when we looked to Fabien's Bend just south of our yard. Virtually every tree in the whole area was either flattened, uprooted or had all its branches from about three or four metres up smashed onto the ground. It was just total devastation. We just could not believe what we saw. Then we went further outside and the only trees not damaged were two gum trees in our yard. Had they fallen or lost branches our house would have been in their path and no doubt smashed down. This was an absolute miracle and we had to thank God for saving us all. The tornado cut a swathe about one kilometre wide right across the bend and up the river.

We then began walking up river to the Hill's house to see how they had fared. Along the river bank there were many big trees and branches blown over into the river. Among the branches in the water were several dozen wet galahs fluttering, some even with broken wings or legs. Among these panicking birds were a number of dead ones and several other desperate birds, like parrots, peewees and crows. It was just so terrible and we could do nothing to help them. We imagined destruction up at the Hills but as we got closer they came to meet us. A corner of their house roof was pulled away and two sheds wrecked and a couple of trees blown over but they were generally safe themselves too. When Dad and Mum described the devastation in the bend and that our house was unscathed they were astonished. We helped pick up many little treasures and papers that blew out of Maudie's damaged room where she had been living.

Each year there was a sports picnic day, generally referred to as "the picnic races" and people living all around Darlington Point attended it. There would be fencers, boundary riders, gardeners, roustabouts and numerous single men. The single men left school to work on stations and were young and keen to show their skills at these picnic days or rodeos. As well there were station families and owners gathering for a day of fun. The young and the old mixed together and they talked about all sorts of things; the weather, the countryside, the seasonal conditions, new people in business or on stations, the unreasonable station managers and whatever.

The day began with a picnic lunch and then a compère would get foot races for various age groups under way, plus games involving the horses. Horse riding games included bending races where riders galloped around drums and put flags in and out of the drums as quickly as possible. Another one involved bareback riders having to jump off their horse, stick their head in a bucket of water and grab a submerged potato, and race back on the horse to a marked spot and continue until their bucket of six potatoes was empty. There were many different challenges for all ages all afternoon, with some using horses and others as individuals or teams. As children we found all this enthralling. Just seeing so many people and horses and listening to the sounds and seeing the movement was so breathtaking compared to the virtually silent life on Wyvern. For days afterwards we talked about the events and how exciting it all was.

On the 30th of August 1947 the Commonwealth Court of Conciliation and Arbitration granted all workers a forty hour week award. Up until then it was a forty four hour week in most industries. This meant that all station hands and workers were entitled to fewer hours per week and in many cases it meant no work for them on Saturdays. This took some adjustment for workers and managers as they rearranged responsibilities and chores. At the same time it gave workers more home time at the weekends.

Being only seven at the time I don't remember much of an impact on our own family routine, other than Dad sometimes having time to go along the riverbank fishing or setting traps for water rats, whose skins were able to be sold.

In October 1946 we had our one and only holiday as a family together. The long drought had broken and the season was good so the manager on Wyvern Station arranged for us to use a family tent they had that was stored with their friends on the coast at Kiama. How excited we were! We had never been on a long train trip before. We had never seen or smelt the sea, or been on a real holiday ever before, so our imagination ran wild! This was all so new.

The train trip was very long but exciting. We put our heads out the windows to smell the lovely burning coal in the steam engines up front. However we got soot in our eyes that stung for a while. We would sit watching, as each telegraph post came and went past the window, with its dozen or so supported wires. The wires would appear to rise and fall, rising at the poles then fall, sagging between poles and rise as the next pole emerged. It was just so fascinating and new for us. There was also the continual clickerty-clack as each set of wheels crossed uneven railway line sleepers, and more so as we crossed little bridges or went through sharp cuttings. The train would stop and start at many railway stations or small sidings along the way and we sometimes got bumped and shaken by the shunting as extra carriages were connected or disconnected.

As we entered Sydney, scenes along the train line impressed us immensely. On both sides of the train lines were huge numbers of little old houses, their rooves all rusty corrugated iron. They had tiny back yards running to the fence below the train tracks. Many yards were bare, others had lots of rubbish in them. We also noticed that there was hardly any greenery or trees anywhere.

A long row of old factory buildings appeared as we rattled past. There were metal gantries and stored stock or what appeared to be unwanted goods stacked high around some big old sheds. It was all so interesting yet horrible looking. We crossed some roads with cars travelling on them and dirty waterways with rubbish in them as we headed for our destination, Central Railway Station. Every few minutes a train would rattle past us, going the opposite way, and so close to our windows we shuddered back in fear because it was so fast and so close.

Eventually we arrived at Central Station in Sydney. The hustle and bustle of people, trains, strange noises and huge buildings just mesmerised us. This was just so overwhelming it frightened us and we were awe struck. Where had the quietness gone? Where were the trees and open space, the smells of nature? This was a whole new world and very scary but then too, so amazingly different to living on Wyvern Station. We just tried absorbing a busy metropolis.

Dad and Mum collected our suitcases and Gladstone bags and the five of us, with me almost seven, Audrey five, and Barbara two, walked up George Street to an old office block around the corner on Pitt Street. Again the mass of people, the noisy trams, buses, cars and coloured taxis was just so overwhelming and awesome. We had never seen anything like this before. We climbed a set of stairs in a doorway and were met in some offices by three or four people. This was the office for Bush Mission Society which Dad and Mum supported and they knew one leader there, Pastor Keith Lynn. After some talking it was lunch time so one man took me down the stairs with him and out into the deafening street to go and buy some sandwiches. I was petrified and soon was left behind. What could I do, where should I go? Then just as suddenly the man arrived by my side and took my hand. What an amazing relief! I then stayed close as we bought lunch and returned up the staircase.

Later that day we returned to Central Station and got on another train and travelled down the coast to Kiama. This time the scenery was more rugged, more densely covered in trees and just so amazingly different to the Riverina. This was an overnight trip and soon it was dark and we fell asleep to the drumming and rattling of the wheels on the tracks and clapping of loose sleepers. Late next morning we disembarked the train and went into a café for lunch. We had fish and chips, another new experience.

By now we were drained of excitement and just very tired. Halfway through the lunch Barbara had a fish bone caught in her throat. After much dry reaching, screaming and assistance from staff the bone was dislodged and Mum was able to pacify her and have her relax. This was not a good start to our holiday. We walked from the café down to a grassed area on the edge of a beach to the pre-arranged large tent. Before long we were set up and ready to explore our surroundings. We three ran down the sand to tentatively dip our toes into the cool ocean for the very first time. How excited we were. We found the sand courser and more yellow than the fine white sand we were used to back home at Fabien's Bend. That was the first of many long hours splashing in the shallows and chasing the tips of the spreading incoming waves.

Later, just along from the tent area we discovered the wonderful site of The Kiama Blowhole. Another new and unforgettable experience for us, as it was just mesmerizing to our little minds. We watched as every few waves brought in a bigger wave that washed into and under the rocks, and then with a thunderous roar shot a jet of water up in the air. This was an incredible site as we tried to figure out which wave would succeed, and how the water shot up like it did and what made it roar anyway. Many times in our week's holiday we went over to watch as the waves rolled in on the rocks. We also loved seeing the sun rise over the sea and spread its light on the caps of the waves. We were in a new and different world and the hours of fun just melted away each day. At the end of the week we returned home in the train. We had so many memories and new experiences, yet no one but ourselves to share them with.

A MOVE TO CALDWELL

THE OWNERS of "Wyvern Station", Sims Cooper, sold out to a Mr T. C. Field in late 1948 and the manager of "Wyvern", Mr Koonahan, who owned a good sheep property near Deniliquin, offered Dad the opportunity to move there and manage it. It was situated about 48 kilometres west of Deniliquin, in a district named Caldwell. This property was called "Comeback Estate". We drove down to inspect it and to see what the home was like. It was a big home and Dad and Mum immediately agreed to take up the position even though it was not on a river and was more than two hundred and fifty kilometres from Griffith.

As children we were excited about moving but really had no idea of the ramifications of such a big move and change. Travelling down through Jerilderie and Conargo was very isolated, flat country. All we saw was the vast Riverina plains with an occasional clump of eucalypt trees, long straight fences, dusty tracks and odd mobs of sheep standing in the hot sun. However, there was something inviting about this country for me, whether perhaps the quietness, or the fact that it varied so much every few kilometres, or the appearance of nature still in control. It just seemed to resonate with me, and still does. We moved there in December 1948.

One not so pleasent memory was the drop toilet down the yard. This lavatory, in the daylight, was like a watchtower or beacon that stood out clean and white but it was scary going to it in the dark because there could be spiders, a snake, eyrie sounds about, or, as we sat on the seat, a deafening silence that gripped you and made you not want to breathe. The "outhouse" as they were generally called, featured a worn wooden seat with a rough shaped hole. If we looked down inside there would be paper, sometimes white worms and even a mouse scurrying up the side. Dad would cut paper into small squares, to use as toilet paper, often using old telephone books for this purpose.

These sheets would be pushed onto a long nail, placed just within reach when required. Each Saturday either Audrey or I in turns had to clean this toilet room. That meant sweeping the walls and floor and using a scrubbing brush with phenyl and then warm water to thoroughly scrub the wooden seat.

Once we settled in to the new life on Comeback Estate there were many things to adjust to. There was still no electricity but there were inside taps and much more space to move around in, both inside and out. It was while living here that we experienced for the first time a refrigerator (kerosene type), a telephone in our house and other "modern conveniences".

With this new job of Dad's came a motor vehicle to travel in. This new vehicle was an ex-army, small Jeep with left hand drive and canvas hood. These Jeeps had no doors, just canvas, and pull down side blinds.

We loved hearing the light rain on the corrugated iron roof; it was so relaxing and a lovely sound when drifting off to sleep. Occasionally a thunder storm would build up in the west. It would grow bigger and darker as it approached, and then there would be thunder and flashes of lightning. We learned to count the seconds after a flash of lightning and each second to the boom of thunder meant roughly how distant away the storm was in miles. Then down would fall big rain drops before a short downpour. The beautiful smell of the ground and dust as the raindrops advanced was fantastic to us. Then as quickly as it came the storm passed then we would go out to find a rainbow. Sometimes just part of the bow appeared, sometimes a dull colour and other times bright colours with a dull second rainbow below it. This was another example of the beauty of nature on the Riverina plains.

We found we had to attend the local school and no longer do correspondence lessons. The Caldwell School was five miles (eight kilometres) from our house and Audrey and I rode there each day. It was a frightening start to our school year having to be at the school by a certain time and to meet and get to know other children. Our previously sheltered life was shattered and it took us some weeks to get to know a routine, listen to and follow the teacher and adjust to the fifteen or so children aged from 5 to 12 years. We had to go to a school assembly every Monday morning, to learn to march in time as a group, to salute a flag and say the National Anthem. It was all scary and different to what we were used to before. I was almost nine and Audrey nearly eight and just riding the eight kilometres each way was tiring. There were two girls in my class and both seemed much brighter than I. In fact I learnt that the teacher always called for an answer from me on a question I didn't know the answer to.

Caldwell Public School comprised a largish single room with wooden desks that seated two students each. On the side of the building was a covered lean-to structure which had a dirt floor and a couple of bench seats and hooks on the wall for school bags and overcoats. Right up the back in each corner of the playground were single toilets, designated "boy" and "girl". We used ink pens, the ink in little ink wells put in holes in the top centre of each desk. Once a week a child was appointed to go around with what was called an ink fountain or a special bottle of ink and pour some carefully into each ink well. In that era everyone was taught to use ink pens carefully and each downward stroke of a letter was wider than the up stroke. This was controlled by how the pen nib was tilted in writing. We had to practice for ages getting the two lines correct.

Inside the main building was an open fireplace with hobs down each side. Parents provided the wood for this fire and the teacher came early to light it to warm the classroom. In winter some children brought homemade pies or waffles and these were put on the hob by the fire at morning break and were hot in time for lunch. To us these were a rare treat and only had on occasions. There was no electricity in those days so no lighting, cooling or heating, apart from the log fire. Most of the other dozen or so children came to school on bikes but sometimes they were driven by a parent or even rode a horse that was tethered in the paddock next door, which was really part of Locksley.

The country schools particularly were involved in certain celebratory events each year. We would get excited the days before these events and often would be asked by the teacher to write an essay or fill out an information sheet. Sometimes there would be a relevant radio broadcast on the battery-operated valve radio to listen to. These features included The Gould League of Bird Lovers which involved a pledge to not harm birds. Each year certificates with our names on them were distributed and sometimes a special badge was given to wear.

Other events our school celebrated included Wattle Day, celebrating the day wattle came out in bloom, the first day of Spring, September 1st, and Arbour Day, remembered in June each year, a day when we often planted trees. Also, about twice a term we would get a delivery of a wooden box of library books that we were encouraged to take home and read. Not many children used them but our family did.

As I mentioned earlier, I had just two girls in my class and I always came third, in fact many times I failed to pass some subjects. This was very embarrassing for me, but the two girls did not in any way belittle me, neither did the teacher for that matter. Later in life I realised that what I thought was painful at the time was really good for me because I learned to trust myself to achieve my goals. I had to accept and learn from it.

Winds were a common influence when riding to and from school. During summer there would be very hot northerlies blowing the whole day. They would dry everything out, create dusty whirlwinds and sometimes even dry our skin so much that it felt like a hard leather layer on our arms and face. Then in winter there could be very strong, cold winds blowing all day from the south. We called these a 'lazy wind' because it felt like they blew right through you instead of going around you. Either season the winds created drying and difficult conditions for man and beast. Breezes in summer kept the wind mills turning to pump water and in winter blew away the fogs and frosts but each had its own peculiar effect on every living thing. The Riverina plains felt the wind roaring across it all year round.

In winter there were, at times, very thick fogs that lasted up until lunch time, or later, and they wrapped around the trees and fences like a thick blanket, vastly reducing visibility. We could only see a few metres in front of us as we rode to school and at times it was very frightening as we tried to keep on the rough gravel road. Sometimes as the fog began to evaporate it would be full of droplets that wet our clothes and everything around us.

There were also severe frosts that made carpets of white as far as the eye could see. Just riding a bike on the tracks or roadways going to school made crackling sounds as the tyres broke the shards of ice in the puddles and table drains. The cold weather associated with frosts caused chilblains on our ears, fingers and feet. They would start out as a strong itch and often red patches and we would put Methylated Spirits on them to dry them out. However often they would develop into large blisters and cause much discomfort for a couple of weeks. Not a nice experience for us in winter.

During the spring we would be attacked by nesting magpies at a certain section of the ride to school. We were really scared each morning as we rode through that part because the magpies would just suddenly swoop at us, barely missing our head. They would loudly click their beaks as they got close to us, and then fly off. There was no way of avoiding them and we hated that section of road for months afterwards. Other birds that enthralled us though were the pelicans and the massive wedge tailed eagles way up in the sky. They would rise up in the thermal draughts and just float for ages, rarely waving a wing. They were so small up there circling slowly around, several at a time, and we thought they were just amazing. We would wonder how they could stay up there and how great it would be to be like them, in total control and getting a bird's eye view of the vast countryside.

About one kilometre from our house was the Caldwell railway siding and near it the Caldwell general store. The railway had a large silo in those days and several farmers brought grain that was stored in the silo. Later, by using a long auger or conveyor it was relayed over to open train trucks. There was also a large sheep yards area with two loading ramps going up from a narrow race to put sheep into double deck railway trucks to be sent to the Melbourne Markets. We called the narrow fenced ramp a 'race' because it was only wide enough for one sheep and often they would run up it thinking it was a way out of the enclosed yard. Dad used this loading or unloading system from time to time for moving stock away from or onto Comeback Estate Station.

The General Store was an interesting place for us as children. It was quite a small shop with a residence behind. The shop was stacked full of groceries and various items for households. It was also the local post office and telephone exchange so was always quite busy. The telephone exchange had a box area with leads on pointed attachments.

When the telephone rang someone picked up a receiver and, after asking the caller who they wanted, the lead was plugged into a socket connecting the caller to that household. Some lines had three or four other households on the same single wire so a Morse code system was used to call the right house using long and short rings. If a storm caused a tree branch to fall on or break the only wire, each farmer had to check the line for the break and report it to the post office. Generally the farmer himself repaired it so other households had connection again.

There were no mail deliveries to the stations and farms in those days, so everyone came to the shop to get their mail. A mail contractor came to the shop from Deniliquin three times a week with mail, parcels and any ordered goods from town, plus fresh bread. At that time there was no such thing as sliced bread. It came in large tank loaves and we had to slice it ourselves. It was great the first day, eating fresh bread with butter and vegemite, or else dripping with salt and pepper on it.

Added services the shop offered included telegrams which were often sent for quick messages rather than using slow letters, and also money orders which were often used instead of cheques. These were cashed at the post office. The shop also sold petrol and various other oil and fuel products. The petrol bowsers were a hand pump system whereby one pulled a handle to pump fuel up into a glass holding reservoir that showed measurements in pints and gallons. Then the petrol was released into the car fuel tank by pulling a trigger on the hose. The store was owned and run by Jack Donovan and his wife Frances and their adult son Russell. Dad would quite often spend quite a lot of time talking to them and we hung around looking at all the things for sale and watching when the phone rang or other local people came in to do business. Common purchases at the shop for our family were small bags of broken biscuits. These were popular for us because we would get all sorts of biscuit pieces, plus small pieces were handy to get a handful.

After a couple of years the owner of Comeback Estate sold the property sold it and we had to move off. We went to a dairy farm on the Murray River, west of Echuca in a district called Wharparilla. The Murray River is some 1600 miles (2575 kilometres) long and before the Hume Dam was completed in 1923 and a number of locks and weirs were built along it, it was known to virtually stop flowing. One such occurrence is recorded as in 1923 it was virtually dry below about Swan Hill.

We were only there on the dairy farm for about six months but I have a couple of strong memories. The rough staff cottage was cold and damp and Mum's health deteriorated living in it. For Audrey and me this was a very new experience because we had to catch a school bus to attend Echuca Primary school. Suddenly we were thrust into a very big school with lots of children and class rooms and a very busy, loud, noisy playground. In the next classroom to mine was a group of disadvantaged, mentally handicapped children of varying ages. They were noisy and sometimes wandered into my classroom and caused problems. It seemed to me the teachers had very little control over them.

One very traumatic incident happened the first afternoon after school. We didn't know which of the several buses we were to catch and we stood back in uncertainty, and suddenly realised our bus had left. After some time of fear a teacher told us to go over the road and ring our parents up. We had no idea what to do and I think we had no money so eventually a shop keeper rang for us. When Dad finished milking he drove in and collected us. By then it was dark. Not a very good start to a new big school experience for two young children.

However one positive experience I remember, was being so close to the Murray River and watching as every week or so a paddle steamer pulling big logs would come up the river. It was great seeing it and hearing the deep thud of the motor driving the steamer and pulling the load up to Echuca wharf.

LOCKSLEY

AFTER ABOUT 6 months of living on the Murray River near Echuca, Dad was offered a new position, managing a sheep property back near our previous school at Caldwell.

This property was owned by an Echuca man, Mr Hayden Berriman who Dad got to know, so we moved later that year. The property was named "Locksley" and had a good home on it and good facilities. The house had huge sugar gum trees along the western and southern fences of the yard and to the east was a hard-base tennis court on which we learnt to play tennis. There was a large chook yard and a single bail cow shed and calf yard nearby.

During winter we loved sitting by the open fire in the lounge room, listening to the battery wireless or reading books under the tall kerosene light with its purring bright mantle glowing. We also had Hurricane Lamps for light. They used kerosene that filtered up through a wick to a little flame that caused a mantle to brightly glow, which created a reasonable light. They were easy to light and economical.

We were certainly glad to get away from the dairy farm and its rough staff house.

Locksley had lots of open country with odd shallow swampy patches with trees and bushes in them. In the timbered areas the sheep congregated during the hotter days, as did many birds. It was in the extensive areas of open country that silence and solitude flourished. One could not hear a sound other than the bike wheels on the dead grass or footsteps if walking. It was just so peaceful. Was it always like this though? No, because over the years the sheep and cattle had trampled the ground hard and eaten off the native grasses and any new tree seedling that dared to germinate. Then the summer thunder storms or heavier winter rains washed the top soil away and carved small gutters that became shallow water courses that, however, saw the water soon evaporate. Man's quest for riches had stolen the lifeblood out of the land. Then along came newly trained agronomists who preached new techniques using minerals and superphosphate and the miracle of irrigation. However rarely did the costs outweigh the benefits in the long term!

Locksley was bisected by the main gravel road that joined the towns of Deniliquin to Barham. The two large paddocks north of this road had the railway line as their eastern boundary. Like most properties or stations, bigger paddocks had names as reference or special feature purposes. The two on north Locksley were named Dougherty's and Tinkler's. The homestead property to the south of the main road had as its western boundary the Wakool to Thule gravel road and its southern boundary the gravelled Thule to Bunnaloo road.

The homestead had a wide front veranda and attractive front door but this was very seldom used. If an insurance salesman or someone walked in from the main road because their car had broken down then they may go to the front door. The yard had a side gate and most people stopped there and walked in to the back door rather than the front. Fortunately our sheep dogs were generally tied up down the yard and could only warn of a visitor by ferocious barking.

Each Saturday we had to work in the house. We would get down on our hands and knees and scrub the linoleum floors and then polish them with a wax. The hallway had a narrow lino runner and along the sides were timber boards we also had to wax. Then too there was cleaning the stove and putting boot polish on it to brighten it and clean out the fireplace as well. Other tasks included cleaning the bath, tidying our rooms and sweeping out the house.

Dad bought a round washing machine with a plunger in it with a handle that pumped the clothes into the water. We had to do much of the pumping. On the side of it was a wringer we turned by hand and we often put too much into it and it jammed. By turning it backwards it generally cleared. The clothes were then put into a tub of clean water with Reckitt's blue and again all was rung out in the wringer. Reckitt's Blue was a popular blueing process to whiten old stained or discoloured clothes and was made by Reckitt and Coleman. Some clothes were starched as well.

Whenever we got bruises or abrasions the first thing to put on them was Zam-Buk. This was a good healing ointment in the 1920s through to about the 1950's. It had an advertising motto of "wonderfully soothing and healing".

HOT SUMMERS

I REMEMBER US being in the umpteenth hot, still day that marks the regular pattern of the January heat waves that hang day after day on the saltbush plains of the Riverina. Every night would be so hot and breathlessly still that we could not sleep well and even the mosquitoes were tired. We woke up at sun up, all drained of energy and enthusiasm. A heat wave sat across the state in early 1951 and we as children lay on the linoleum floor in the hallway after lunch each day trying to keep cool. The temperature hovered around 116 degrees Fahrenheit or 46.5 Celsius.

For over a week it was around this temperature and the nights were nearly as bad. It just drained us all with no cool air flowing or ways to get properly cool. Heatwaves lasting one to two weeks were common across the Riverina, in almost every year, particularly during January and February. I remember seeing waves of hot air shimmering on the plains like thin water dancing on the ground in the distance.

A YOUNGSTER'S OBSERVATIONS

AS I SAT on our shady back verandah on a hot day, I took in the beauty of nature around me. I looked up into the tall gum trees surrounding our home and saw their stretched out branches and pale green leaves, all hanging down.

I knew these trees were home to many birds. I noticed, for example, that crows, magpies and parrots chose to build nests in little forked branches, while others like kookaburras and hawks preferred a hollow in a large limb or trunk. Other birds use the higher branches to see the landscape or watch for predators or food sources. I thought about other tree dwellers I have seen here, possums, and goannas and in certain season's bats and even snakes or rabbits around their roots.

I looked up into the sad looking hanging leaves and in a moment my thoughts wandered again. Some years the trees have lovely blossoms and out of these come lots of lovely little gum nuts. The varying seasons make varying amounts of blossoms, from sparse to prolific. I wondered how the various species of honeyeaters know when to come and feast on the nectar in the blossoms. These majestic trees are a rich source of food, shelter and nesting opportunities for so many birds, animals and insects.

Just past the gum trees is a little dry dam. There are numerous gum trees further away on a dry water course that only flows after heavy rain in just some winters. As I sat and swiped away a constant torment of little house flies I began to lazily think. Why don't these flies find the heat as annoying as I do? Why don't they go away to some quiet, cooler spot in a log or limb? But no, they are content in pestering me and landing all over me, finding drops of perspiration and salty moisture to drink and thrive on. They are busy and happy and obviously have told their families to come and share the spoils. They think I am their best friend as they fight to get up close and personal.

My mind continued to wander as I sat in the heat.

In fact over around that dry creek bed there are, in several places, old fallen trees and branches. Some look like they have lain in this position for many years. Actually in places new trees are growing up between the rotting limbs to continue the cycle of regeneration. How amazing these giants of beauty and grandeur have a new family growing up before them. This cycle has been growing here for hundreds, even thousands, of years. What stories they could tell, of droughts and floods, extremes of heat and cold and they just quietly live on. They have stood against wind storms and whirlwinds and the occasional loss of a limb or two or felt the shuddering vibration as a nearby tree has fallen or been blown over, but they quietly live on.

I began thinking about the bark on these Red Gum trees. How I often used to pull large sheets off and see insects and spiders under them. Also holes bored into the trunk. I used number 8 fencing wire with a curved tip to push into the holes, twist it and pull out a large white grub. Sometimes when the nearby big dam was partly full I would use these grubs for bait to catch a fish. Suddenly I was awakened back to reality by the cough from our dog who was laying asleep in a hollowed out patch in the dirt a couple of feet away from me.

It was still very hot and eerily still. No sound, no breeze, just the clammy close feeling of heat and more heat. I realised I was thirsty so I reached up to the water bag hanging on a bent wire, hooked at the other end through a hole in the iron roof. The water was not cold, just cool, and didn't really quench my thirst but there was no alternative. I screwed the top off our water bag, took a pannikin and had a slow drink. I moved myself a few inches, spoke a few words to Gunner and we both settled back to our day dreaming.

We named our dog Gunner, because Dad kept hoping that one day he was "gunner" be a good dog. But we somehow kept hoping. He was a part Kelpie, part mongrel who kept close to us all the time but who didn't like working with sheep, or even obeying instructions for that matter. But we were good mates. He didn't like all the heat either so spent his time lying around and sleeping. However if we went walking along the creek bank he would be up in an instant and would start darting in and out around the logs and branches sniffing for rabbits or goannas. It seemed he suddenly had plenty of energy, but if he couldn't find anything, he would slowly lope back and follow close behind us hoping something exciting might soon happen.

DROVERS

ON THE ROADS around Caldwell and all around the Riverina there were drovers with sheep or occasionally a mob of cattle. In the drier times some station owners would pay drovers to take some of their livestock along the roads and stock routes. Their task was to keep the mobs together, make sure they were safe, guide them to food and water and eventually bring them back home. Or they may take them to pre-arranged saleyards when advised by the owner.

Many of the men and women drovers were "losers" who for various reasons did not like town life. However, there were other drovers who were very professional and always in demand by stock owners. Drovers characteristically travelled in big, old, horse drawn wagonettes, frequently referred to as "rough turnouts". These were low, canvas covered swing cart style, often with four rubber tyres. Under the floor were crates the dogs stayed in. They carried drums of water and appeared overloaded with wire, dogs and bits and pieces.

Water was often a problem on the road, there being long distances between dams, wells or creeks. So they carried drums with them for drinking and cleaning. For this reason to some their motto was the old proverb, "If he doesn't wash his hands he is dirty and if he does he is wasting water". There were generally six or more dogs following along, under or beside the wagonette, and some were tied to the gear so as not to chase the mob, or wander off. They were normally a mixed pack of dogs and only some were reliable enough to control the stock or push the stragglers into action.

Drovers normally had one particular horse they used every day as they moved along. This was a very quiet horse, trained to walk slowly or mooch along behind the scattered sheep as they fed. The drover would go criss-cross along the rear of the mob and quietly hurry up any straggler getting behind the rest. Sometimes the stragglers could be unwell or just needing encouragement to keep up with the main group of sheep. At times a sheep or lamb may injure a leg stepping over a piece of wood, or log, or bruise it in an unseen gilgie hole in the grass and so begin limping behind. This horse knew to get up close to the offending sheep and be so close the sheep would scamper or hobble forward to the others up ahead, just for safety.

The men were generally unshaven, roughly dressed and used profane words in most sentences to impress a tone, or to emphasise their conversations to their listeners. They would at times be like Abraham and Abimelech in the Bible, quarrelling over the rights to, or possession of a bore or dam and who arrived there first etc. They generally had two or three extra staff with them, and occasionally one had a wife with him, and most of these women were just as rough as the drover himself. Many drovers were "old codgers", passed their prime but they enjoyed their job and had no other reason to retire or even know where to retire.

The drover's routine was standard. The Bushman's Clock would wake them. The bushman's clock was a common name for Kookaburras. They begin laughing or calling even before the first glimpses of sunrise appear and call back and forth to each other in the trees. So at first light the cook or chief drover would stir up the camp fire, prepare boiling hot tea and fresh damper and set out extra food for the drovers to take in their bags on their horses. After breakfast he cleaned up and then would move ahead, stopping to set up the billy for lunch time, then go on to the overnight camp.

The main meals consisted of meat, onions, potatoes or rice, tinned fruit or vegetables. Curry and spices masked stale ingredients or mistakes. Bully Beef was a common food for most drovers. Bully beef was made from the brisket or front part of the cow and was corned or cured in large lumps or corns of salt and left to dry out somewhat. Thus it would keep for several days. Jam and treacle were the main sweet, which were mostly eaten on damper. They were generally allowed one beast per week to kill and eat from their mob but each had to be recorded just as were any deaths of their stock on the road trip.

In most cases an all night watch had to be kept over the cattle, because a rush was the most feared thing by drovers. This was when a noise, or no real reason even, the cattle would all bolt off.

"When a mob go, they go bang, that's it, and you was dead asleep and you would just jump up straight out, no boots, straight onto the night horse and you were gone", acording to Scotty Watson, an old cattle drover.

It was the drover's job to try to turn the cattle into a circle and let them run themselves out. Chasing cattle through rough country in the dark was a nightmare though. However if it were sheep they were much more docile and needed less care at night, although foxes and wild dogs could be a problem. If there were no fences in the area close to where they camped for the night sometimes drovers tied three or four dogs on long chains across the area so at night the sheep would not wander.

There were numbers of wide road strips or travelling stock routes throughout the Riverina. These travelling stock routes were often several hundred metres wide so stock could spread out to eat. Occasional places on the stock routes had fenced holding yard areas and sometimes a bore or dam as watering places. The water was rather terrible and very muddy in some of these dams. In fact drovers used to claim that at times if they used the water in a whistling kettle the kettle would cough instead of whistle.

The famous Riverina stock route is the Long Paddock, a wide route from Echuca (Moama side of the Murray) up through Deniliquin and Hay to Hillston. The government had conditions of travel with livestock, sheep had to travel 6 miles (9.5 kilometres) per day and cattle 10 miles (16 kilometres). This was to stop the countryside being eaten bare and devastated by over stocking. Some station managers did not like drovers passing by their property, particularly in very dry times. They would accuse the drover of bringing weeds or burrs along their boundary or at times they claimed the drover allowed his mob to force themselves over or through the boundary fence for better food or water.

Drovers would have half a dozen horses with them to control the mob and these required care with food and water. Many drovers had a bell that they tied to a horse at night so they knew where the horse was next morning. These bells were often the sought after Condamine Bell because they were heard clearer and a longer distance away, than other made bells. Also some horses were fitted with hobbles to their front feet at night so they could not wander far. The chain-like metal hobbles were like hand cuffs and restricted the separate movement of their front legs so making the horse do little jumps to move around.

Many drovers whiled away their hours by repairing their gear, whether horse saddles or bridles or their own boots, hats and whips. They used strips of leather as mending material and would plat it such as for whips, or soften it in boiling water and create patches or covers. They would use long steel needles and pinches or pliers to pull the leather into place and then stitch it down to make a long lasting repair. Some drovers made whips and others carved patterns into the leather to build skills that made them important characters when visiting a town or local pub along the road. Some even sold their masterpieces for small monetary gain to supplement their living costs when things were tough and there was no work about.

After about three years Mr Hayden Berriman sold Locksley to an adjoining neighbour to the north, a Mr Eric Brookesby who wanted Dad to stay on and run the property, which was excellent news for all of us.

RABBITS

LIGNUM BUSHES GROW as large spiked shrubs in the low flat areas along the waterways and creeks, particularly along the Wakool River. Each bush is generally quite widespread and sheep avoid them. This creates a quiet living area for birds and insects and the rabbits find safe living areas under them too, particularly as they are generally close to permanent water holes.

These were Dad's special rabbit chasing areas on a Saturday. He would take Audrey and I shooting and we would come home with a dozen or so to either sell as meat or for their skins. This was particularly the case in the early 1950's when rabbit meat was popular. Twice a week a rabbit buyer would travel through picking up bodies either at homesteads or left in hessian bag covers at certain pick up points in a tree or crate by the main road. He would leave money in a container when he collected and counted the gutted, unskinned carcases. The rabbits were hung by their hind legs in pairs across a piece of stick with their backs outwards.

Rabbit traps were used on every farm or station. These were steel traps with two jaws that quickly snapped together when a rabbit stood on them. To set a trap, a flat area was chipped out just below the ground surface. By putting one's foot on the base of the jaws they would open out flat and then a little clip kept them open. Between the jaws was a loose flat piece of light steel, the tongue, and over it was put a small piece of paper to stop soil and sand getting under it. Then the tongue and flat jaws were covered in a thin layer of soil to completely hide the trap. Attached to the end of the trap was a chain, about 70 centimetres long, and the other end had a steel peg tied to it. This peg was driven into the ground so the caught animal could not run off with the trap. Rabbit traps were cruel but effective. Sometimes a stray cat, a fox, or a hare would be caught. Sometimes too, the rabbit would run round and round and its foot would break off and it would escape. This would be a painful result for the poor thing. These traps were generally set at the mouth of rabbit burrows or in dung hills, an area where male or buck rabbits generally went to dispose of their little balls of dung.

However a more cruel destruction of the rabbit plague was when in about 1950 the mosquito and flea bearing virus Myxomatosis was introduced to Australia. 'Myxo', as it was called, was a disease that quite quickly killed the rabbits. However, before dying, over a period of about two weeks, they developed skin tumours or lumps along their backbone, swelling around the eyes, then blindness and severe fever. It was a cruel suffering disease and some rabbits looked terrible as they struggled to hop away from us. If we caught or shot a rabbit with any indication of Myxo we could not sell the animal and often even the skin was not worth removing. It was claimed the rabbit population across Australia reduced from six hundred million to one hundred million in two to three years from late 1950.

Black Fellow's (Fellas) Ovens or Aboriginal ovens or middens are found near the creeks and lagoons, particularly along the Wakool River. They cover from about two metres by two metres, to in some places, about five metres by five metres. They are a patch of flattened black charcoal mixed with a dirt base with some having mussel shells and small bones in them. They are often twenty to forty centimetres deep. Trees do not grow in them but over the years of not being used they tend to flatten out and the grass grows up around the edges. Rabbits use them to burrow in and under.

There were times when I would set eight or ten rabbit traps to catch rabbits for money, either by selling their carcasses or just their skins. I would set them in the afternoon in known rabbit areas in a paddock then go around them after dinner and again next morning. Some nights it was quite scary travelling down the paddock on my own. I had a rather dull torch on my bike and maybe I would suddenly come across cows or sheep quite close by, because the torch didn't shine far, or I may frighten a bird or owl as I rode under a tree. It would suddenly fly off and scare me. Another time I might hear bush curlews screeching their awfully weird cries to each other and they would make the hairs on my neck stand up. Other times there might be a scary noise from a nearby, yet hidden, Spur-winged Plover (or Masked Plover). They have a loud noise and in the day time often swoop down on us, so just their sound scared me in the dark. Yet other causes of fear might be a fox or wild cat caught in a trap and I had to find a strong stick to kill it to get it out of a trap. I would then ride home and skin any rabbit while it was still warm and hang its skin over a rabbit bow or gut it if I was to sell it.

A rewarding part of rabbit trapping was the scenery at night as I rode my bicycle or reset a trap. Just to look up into the sky on a cloudless and moonless night was like magic. To see the millions of little stars closely fitting together in the vast sky was amazing. Particularly special was the Milky Way, a swathe or vast pathway of stars that looked milky or not really clear because it was so far away in the sky. There were odd brighter stars but not many in the whole Milky Way. Many would twinkle and when I focussed on where I saw one twinkle it would not twinkle again, it just glistened in the dark background.

Then on a moonlight night, especially around a full moon, I could see across the paddock so clearly and I didn't need the torch switched on while riding along the track. Everywhere was crystal clear light and under the trees it was a glowing patchwork of different shades of light. I would be shut out of sounds and just mesmerised by the different lights and the myriads of stars, it was so magical to behold. A slight breeze might send the quaint smell of a blossom or the strong odour of a nearby fox but all this was overcome by the beauty of the night. There might be a quiet call from a far away Mopoke Owl or the eerie call of a Curlew, but I quietly went on with my rabbit trapping, still transfixed by the Milky Way and starry sky above. This was nature at its best, enjoyed by me alone, in the Riverina bush and on the edge of the saltbush plains.

When setting traps I would sometimes come across a small perfectly round trapdoor on the ground about the size of a five cent piece. This was the door to a trapdoor spider's home, just a tiny door that protected it from being captured by a watchful bird. These spiders were light brown and scary looking with hairy legs and a set of tiny fangs at the front, so I avoided getting near them.

THE SHEEP INDUSTRY

BECAUSE DAD WAS employed on large sheep stations he learned all about sheep husbandry. The usual practice for sheep breeding was to put the station rams in with the mobs of female sheep, ewes, just for a time, often 2 months. In that time most ewes were fertilised and so dropped their lambs in a common two month period, taking on average 147 days to gestate.

When it came time for lamb marking, all the lambs in a mob were of similar age so later on could be sold as a job lot of similar production. The marking process was for each lamb to be caught and put up on its buttock on a rail on the sheep yard fence. A hand punch type apparatus put an identification hole in the left hand ear, or some stations used the right ear. Then their tail was cut off at the second joint with a sharp knife. If the lamb was a male normally the testicles were removed by cutting the scrotum with a knife and pulling the testes away using a pincher type of hand held pliers. Some men preferred to use their teeth to do this instead. A dab of disinfectant was put on the scrotum and tail base and they were returned to the pen of waiting mothers.

Some years later a change in procedure was common for the castrating of male lambs and the removal of their tails. There came into popular use green rubberised bands called Elastrators that were put over the base of the tail and the scrotum using a special applicator. These bands stopped the blood circulation and within about three weeks the tail and bag would fall off and the skin at the base would be completely sealed over. A couple of months later when the lambs were about six months to eight months old they were again yarded and many then put into a separate yard and a truck would take them to a local town sheep sale, in Deniliquin, Barham or Echuca.

The actual butchering or killing of sheep and cattle on stations for meat is a quick death. Whether in small yards or at station slaughter pens, it is quick and final compared to the long term suffering of these animals through drought, thirst, starvation, flood, fire or disease. In fact many farmers suffer alongside their animals because they see the pain and suffering their livestock experience in these times of disaster. Statistics for stock losses are intertwined with the term 'struggles with nature'. Every generation of station owners sees times of suffering for their stock.

In a drought time sheep will scratch areas of ground to find seeds, or roots of plants, to keep them going, or will stand on tip toe to pull down tree leaves. Sheep and cattle will push over fences to get into other areas in the hope of finding food. Eventually they become so weak they lay on the ground and crows fly down, take out their eyes and wait until they die. Then with the eagles they will feast on their carcases. We saw this first hand from time to time and ached for the suffering sheep. The death of one animal or a bird means food for another animal or bird. This applies to the death of rabbits or other pests destroyed by man or predators too, and they then become food for smaller life like hawks, flies or worms.

Much of the moving of sheep and cattle between markets and the stations was done by drovers. Drovers often had mobs of over 1,000 head of cattle and up to 3,000 with sheep. After the Second World War trucks began moving stock and these 'steering wheel drovers' caused many drovers to lose their jobs.

When a season is wet and sheep are carrying a lot of wool they have another problem at lambing time. They lay down to rest and if they happen to be in a small hollow in the ground or are a little weak carrying a lamb and have lots of wool and it rains, they can easily be unable to regain their footing and get up. Again crows are watching and if farmers do not see them lying down in time, the crows kill them by removing an eye and piercing their body with their beak.

Shearing on Locksley and Mr Brooksby's other two properties was done in late winter. The shearers would then come back around February to crutch all the sheep. The shearers who came to Locksley were a gang of five to seven aboriginal or part aboriginal men from Barmah. Barmah is a small village on the bank of the New South Wales side of the Murray River but recorded as being a town in Victoria because of the bend in the river. On the New South Wales side an aboriginal settlement was established about 1905 and was named Cummeragunja. This area is some 35 kilometres upstream from Moama and Echuca and is renowned for being near the largest red gum forest in the world, the Barmah State Forest. This forest floods periodically and is a breeding ground for Murray Cod and other fish and a popular area for bird life.

Most of these aboriginal shearers each season were good workers, clean and reliable. They would sleep in the shearers hut, a three bedroom long galvanised shed type building between the house and the shearing shed. It had a joint kitchen dining room but the men had all their meals in our house. Mum had to cook them a hot breakfast, lunch and dinner, plus morning and afternoon tea and have it always ready right on time. She had a wood stove only and a tiny kitchen and a dish, not a sink, to wash up in.

Dad would be busy in the shed but come to the house to help get all the food ready and set the table on time. Shearing usually lasted two weeks, but sometimes went a few extra days, particularly if there were wet days. Crutching was usually a one week operation. Crutching involved cutting an area clean around the sheep's belly button and removing all wool from around the backside of the sheep to stop fly blowing. Generally one or two from Brooksby's other properties came to help yard sheep, press wool into bales and help make the many tasks easy for all concerned.

Sheep have strong lanolin in their wool and this gives an oily cover, over time, on shearing shed fences, as well as inside and outside the sheds, the floor boards where they are shorn, and on the shearer's boots and their long trousers and singlets. It was a tradition that shearers generally wore grey flannelette singlets.

When moving sheep from say one paddock to another or to the shearing shed or yards, they could become very obstinate, particularly near a gateway or up a ramp. They stand looking at you and stamp a foot or turn and run back into the main mob, or they take off in a mob racing down a fence line avoiding looking back even when a dog tries to turn the leaders back. Other times they stand in a pack and the outside ones run around the pack protecting the main mob and refusing to break and go forward. When being driven along a fenced road they will run for ages before being stopped just to avoid going in a gateway that they should go in. Some people said "the only thing madder than sheep are the blokes that work them".

About the beginning of the 1950's wool became a very rich source of income because ridiculous prices were being paid by overseas milliners. In fact for a time one pound weight of wool was getting one pound in money. We would collect pieces of wool left by sheep where they rubbed themselves on fences or gather wool off the ground where a sheep had died some time back. Dad would bag it up and take it to Browns in North Deniliquin and get paid good money for it.

THE ADVANCE OF AGRICULTURE

IN 1949, after the Second World War, returned soldiers were allocated land as soldier settlers along the Murray River in areas around Swan Hill and upstream around Cobram. The State governments provided the land by ballot and the Commonwealth government the sponsored loans. It took a lot of blood, sweat and tears though to get to having viable food producing farms.

Most of these ex-soldiers had limited farming experience; they lacked equipment and were unfamiliar with rural life. They had to combat rabbits and other pests plus a lack of irrigation water because the government was terribly slow in their promised irrigation works. They spent long days watering their newly planted fruit trees or seedlings by hand, a very tedious job. Then some didn't want irrigation channels in or near their property because they feared their small children may drown. But the channels eventually came through and some of these new farmers received wages for helping build them. Another issue was poor surveying and in some place channels actually went slightly uphill rather than level so extra wages were available to remedy the problem.

Certain water rights were allocated to properties and this was gauged by using a formula of a certain depth of water to cover one acre of land. Each outlet from the main channel had a water wheel on it. This was a large black wheel with fins on it. On its axle was a small metre gauge that recorded each revolution of the wheel. Water flowed through an adjustable metal gate and this flow turned the wheel sending measured water down the farmer's main channel.

Fences were erected to subdivide paddocks and the government subsidised the costs of boundary fences facing public roads and stock routes. It was to the government's benefit that the farmer did the work and protected the boundary fences. Fences were erected perfectly straight as far as the eye could see and without using a theodolite. They put in two steel posts about 5 metres apart and lined both up with a distant fence post so that the steel post closest to that distant post was hidden by the other steel post. Then a strong straight box tree post was rammed into a pre dug hole. Between each wooden post was a distance of 10 to 15 metres and several steel posts were hammered in between the wooden posts. Then wires pulled through, a barbed wire on top, and the fence completed.

In the Riverina there are many varieties of plants and flowers. Their growth depends on the soil types and the different seasons. In fact some flowering plants only appear every fifteen or twenty or so years when a season of rain or temperature is just right for their germination and growth. Then they will appear prolifically in some paddocks and be so picturesque. It is amazing that through flood or drought those seeds are sitting in the subsoil just waiting for the perfect season. They include bluebells, paper daisies, yellow buttercups, barley grass, corkscrew, scotch thistles, or weeds, like Bathurst burrs, or cat head prickles.

Stinging nettles were another that grew in clumps when a season was right. These would be up to thirty or forty centimetres high, bright green with large leaves and if they touched your skin it caused an itchy sting for up to an hour. It was amazing that just quite suddenly these different native plants would appear and show off their beauty and colour. It was in this country, the Riverina, where I learnt about God's creation of beauty and wonder. As a boy growing up it was this that moulded my perspective of nature in the life of those river flats and vast plains. There is such a brilliant life and culture in the land of the Riverina and out of it grows so many amazing things.

Roly Poly is a round noxious weed that grows as a bush and that animals do not eat. It has a short life span then dies off in the spring. Wind blows them and they roll across the paddocks and pile up in packs along fences, in water troughs and channels, or against fallen trees. They tend to grow mainly in degraded country and soil with a clay base. They have curly tendrils with five spikes on each so easily catch onto wire netting fences. In bush fires they are a good feed for fires and cause fence posts to ignite thus causing lots of costly damage to farmers.

Another large plant that grows in the Riverina is the Dillon Bush. These large bushes are shaped like upturned bowls and have branches all the way around that reach to the ground. They generally grow on salty flat soil in groups and are popular for rabbits to hide in. They are thick enough to hold blowing dust and are seldom eaten by stock, thus they are a nuisance in paddocks.

Waterways, farm dams and irrigation channels get filled by a large spindly plant called Cumbungi. This plant also is not eaten by stock. Cumbungi has a big tuber like root that is hard to dislodge and develops other tubers that over a couple of years spread throughout the mud in the water. Cumbungi impedes water flow and creates a nuisance for farmers with irrigation channels. It has long flat strap like reeds that have sharp edges and each can be nearly a metre long. It has large brownish flowers on long stems. Aboriginals used the leaves for weaving and the roots were crushed for flour. Water birds, particularly water hens, nest in them profusely.

During the hotter weather there would be an occasional whirly wind, or willy willy, or dust devil, that cut across a paddock. It would gather dust and dead grass and leaves "into a giant ice-cream cone, twirling and whistling as it spun on its tail and leave debris as a reminder of its brief visit".[5]

They are similar to tornados but on a miniature scale and can cause local damage in their path. They would whirl around picking up dust and grass and quite suddenly just disappear across the paddock.

The differing weather conditions each season affected various natural phenomena. There might be one year for just a week when thousands of moths would appear, generally blown along by the wind. They would get into everything and once inside

---

5 *In the Middle of Nowhere* by Terry Underwood, p.77. First published in hardcover in 1998 by Bantam, paperback edition in 1999 by Bantam.

our house would get into bed linen, under anything they could and annoy us at night around our lamps.

Another year it might be a couple of days when flying ants would drive us mad. They would appear from nowhere and get into everything.

Other years it might be locusts or grass hoppers as they were called then, that would eat every blade of grass, whether green or brown. Then another time it might be cicadas or the wind might blow thousands of rollie pollies or umbrella grass against fences and logs. Then another year there might be midges all night, or swarms of tiny insects. The natural changes in weather conditions create new and differing effects on life in the Riverina from year to year.

Locksley only had an old rough Landrover to do work around the property in. Then Eric Brookesby bought Dad a new 1951 FX Holden, cream in colour and the registration number was ABK 791.

It was amazing, it had a hard roof, not canvas and glass windows that wound down. We thought we were just the ultimate as passengers. This was soon after Holden brought out their first utilities. About 1955 he replaced it with a 1954 Holden utility registration number GLU 770. When we went into Deniliquin I always had to sit in the back because there was not enough room inside the cab. The tonneaux cover would be pulled up over the back and clipped onto studs. If cold or showery I was completely covered inside it.

Dust would enter from the rear and it was terribly rough sitting on the bare metal floor or an old wheat bag. Once when coming home we struck a thunderstorm and twice lightning struck the ground about one kilometre in front of us and as we got closer grass fires started in the grass on the side of the road. Often these would start by striking the many beer and soft drink bottles thrown out over the years by passing motorists or left by drovers. Generally the accompanying rain put the fires out or the wet grass soon overwhelmed them.

YANCO AGRICULTURAL HIGH SCHOOL

AT THE BEGINNING of 1952 our family received a letter stating that I had won a bursary to attend Yanco Agricultural High School. This was exciting for us because it meant no struggling with Correspondence lessons and joining with like minded students at a school that majored on agriculture studies. So with bags packed I was taken into Deniliquin, boarded a bus to Jerilderie and waited there for a little passenger train from Tocumwal to take me to Narrandera. Once there I was picked up in a small covered in truck, owned by the school, and taken out to the school, near the village of Yanco.

The school had a huge two story old building that was like a dormitory type sleeping quarters and various class rooms. There was a sports ground and various agricultural areas such as a big dairy, horse stables, market garden area, small sheep paddocks and various machinery sheds and silos.

However a sudden realisation hit me hard. Here I was with around two hundred other students in a controlled environment. I knew no one. I had to adjust to time constraints, certain rules, lots of teachers who didn't connect to us and lots of more senior students who treated first years with disdain and force. I soon found out about an initiation night the first week when all first years had to sing or do some type of entertainment in front of the whole school and many of the teachers. What could a very shy boy like me do? I got a loan of a mouth organ and attempted to play a tune that I had tried to learn but failed at when living at home. After several notes I was booed off. Fortunately other first year efforts were failures and booed too.

As the first term progressed I realised I was a poor student and the lessons were hard to understand and mostly beyond me. I would go through periods of loneliness, depression, fear of failure and fear of the control of senior students. Myself and other first years were forced up into a half full grain silo and made to strip to our underpants and run around inside until we nearly collapsed. Other times we were made to go down near the fence around the market garden which was supposed to be out of bounds for school attendees. The seniors would climb through the fence and take fruit, or water melons and we had to "keep nits" or watch out if the staff were coming. If the seniors were caught we were blamed and punished.

There were times when many of the students could go swimming after school hours in the Murrumbidgee River that formed part of the school property boundary. However senior students would harass a couple of first years, take their clothes, throw the clothes up in tree and send them back to school just in underpants.

At night up to a dozen boys slept in each room of the residence and once lights went out there was to be no noise. Often someone would make some sounds and when the teacher on duty came in the older boys always said it was a first year that did it. One teacher had a wide belt and he metered out punishment by making the suspected guilty boy stand at the end of his bed and bend over and he received two or three hard wacks with the belt onto his backside. Other teacher punishments for us first years were emu parades, going around the grounds collecting papers and rubbish, and being seen by teachers and students as bad offenders for some misdemeanour.

These acts of terror and ridicule made my life even harder to bear and having no parent nearby to console with was even harder. At the end of each term it was going home for two weeks that was also hard. I didn't want to appear as a sook or defeatist and I didn't want to return to face more of the humiliation. This was a "from" Locksley "to" loneliness situation for me. We could not telephone each other and letter writing was not common in those times. This was a long, hard, lonely year for me.

I sometimes was rostered on to help with milking. I would be up out of bed around four in the morning and given a torch by the dairy man in charge and go out across paddocks in the dark to bring the milkers in. They were good cows but it was a little daunting out in the paddocks when there was no moon. Then I helped milk using mechanical cups on the cows.

I was still extremely light for my age and weighed, from memory, just over 4 stone (about 28 kilos). I got very ill at one time and the medical sister at the school was worried about me having an extremely high temperature. She began me on a twice daily dosage of malt extract and cod liver oil. I took this for a couple of months and increased my weight quite considerably for which I was very grateful.

Then to cap it off in third term my parents received a letter stating there had been a mistake and I had not qualified for the bursary. I was never sure if my parents read the first letter wrongly, not noting certain conditions, or if there really was a genuine mistake, but the school allowed me to complete the year. However I failed most of the exams in the final assessments anyway.

So the next year I repeated 7th class and my sister Audrey was now in the same class year. We both began the high school years by correspondence from Sydney. Because we lived within one mile of a public school the law required we attended that school and did the lessons under the supervision of the teacher in charge. Caldwell school was about one kilometre from our house so we had to comply.

This was not an ideal situation to learn in or get help because it was a one teacher school and Mr Durante had some 15 pupils in all classes from kindergarten to sixth to spend all his time with. As a result there was very little care for us doing high school and this caused little motivation to advance. Younger needy children were the teacher's prime concern and also the teacher was not trained for higher education requirements over primary school subjects, particularly writing and maths.

There were annual events we went to as a school, like district small school sports days but because Audrey and I were doing high school work and older than children in the other half a dozen schools, we were not really involved. There were also various special events like planting trees on Arbour Day, or the annual end of year Christmas party and school presentation which we were involved in. There were occasional visits to the school by a church minister to conduct scripture, and the local State Government Minister, Mr Joe Lawson.

Mr Lawson was a parliamentary member for a number of years and the extension of the Irrigation Scheme to the west of Deniliquin (The Deniboota Scheme) was pushed to success by him. Deniliquin is on the Edward River, a 383 kilometre anabranch of the Murray River. The main water pipeline had in fact had to go under the Edward River at Deniliquin and a siphon system was installed. The Syphons consisted of two concrete barrels, 3.6 metres in diameter and 700 metres long going under the Edward River and nearby Aljoes Creek to take water from the huge Mulwala Canal to the new irrigation area west of Deniliquin and out to places including Caldwell. It was officially opened on Wednesday 27th of April, 1955. This was named as The Lawson Siphon after him. Whenever he visited our school we had to practice etiquette and respect before hand, and thoroughly clean up the playground and classroom. As a result he always gave us a designated day off school, for which we all felt honoured.

From about the age of twelve I often wished I had a pup or dog of my own. This desire increased as I went through my early teens. Dad had three sheep dogs and I wished I had one that was mine.

About this time my sister Audrey got a horse. Often after school and on weekends she would spend hours talking to it, feeding it straw and riding it. Sometimes when riding it though, the horse would get very strong willed and canter all round the paddock.

As well my younger sister Barbara would be given orphaned or sick lambs. She would feed them using a beer bottle with teat added. They would rush up to the fence at her call and demand with waggling tails to be fed.

Occasionally one of Dad's dogs would give birth to several beautiful little playful and cuddly pups. I would spend hours with them and choose one as my possible, permanent pet.

Whether Dad thought I would not feed it every day or whether he did not want to have another dog on the property I am not sure. I would come home from school, go down to the kennels and all the pups would come out. However one day I would go and find all the pups missing. Dad had killed off the whole litter, so no pup for me again. I would be angry and very sad but no explanation or reason would be given to me.

I must say Dad never to my knowledge ever said he was proud of me in anything or that he loved me. He was one who sometimes talked a little about topics but never about feelings. Topics were safe and superficial whereas issues could be evocative and heart to heart or expressing strong personal feelings.

It was about this time Dad had a little spare money and bought a tall cabinet, with a battery operated radio and a turntable to play records. The records were small 45's and long play 33's and a third, but Dad hardly ever bought any. However the radio was used a lot and it was the programmes he listened to that got me interested in country music which was what he liked. I loved listening to the cowboy songs that were popular then. As well he began buying regular cartoon books, namely Jolliffe's editions of Witchetty's tribes that made fun of aboriginal life and also Jolliffe's Saltbush Bill that made fun of life on a farm in the old days. They came out about once a month and were quite funny.

Opposite the school was a small, corrugated iron, community hall and two tennis courts. About two Sundays a month a minister from the Baptist Church in Barham came and took a service in the hall. We also had a Sunday school. Probably about 10 adults attended the service and about the same number the Sunday school. One couple brought a tiny pump peddle organ for music. Everyone dressed up for church, men in ties and ladies wore hats.

At times the hall was used for dances and concerts. I remember the odd times we attended a dance and generally there would be a good attendance as it was a social time for everyone. It was a friendly night and most dances were traditional ballroom style.

However when the new teacher came, a Mr Knox Durante in the early 1950's, he taught us children square dancing and this became a part of the hall dancing programme. The local women organised a vast array of goodies for the supper break.

A small group of older men came along but seldom got up to dance. They sat together in a corner just inside the entrance door. They would slowly roll their cigarettes and enjoy a drink from their large brown glass, beer bottles as they gossiped away. All of them had baggy trousers held up by braces and they wore big boots. These "old codgers" as Mum called them or "old fellas" as Dad called them would spend the night discussing the weather, the sheep and wool prices, who had improved their farm and many trivial subjects.

These old timers seldom went further than our nearest towns and had been on the same farm for many years, however they had perseverance and common sense and the most important thing in life for them was staying the course, finishing the race, beating the ravages of the Riverina climate, and avoiding taxes. They worked hard every day and their hardened hands, and their worn bodies showed their determined passion to stick it out whatever the cost. I admired them and wished I could sit and learn from them but as a young lad I was not welcomed into their world those evenings.

When we went to socials or dances in the hall there seemed to always be one last event and it involved virtually everyone. The Master of Ceremonies would call up everyone to join hands in a big circle around the edge of the dance floor. The pianist would play the old Scottish song Auld Lang Syne and everyone would sing the first verse and chorus while holding hands. This was quite embarrassing for me because they made mostly alternate male and females to stand together. I might have to hold the hand of some older person I didn't even know. Then as the chorus was sung some would let go and put their hands across their chest for some reason. Once the last note was sung everyone, while still holding hands rushed into the centre, kicked up one leg then went back out to the edge. Then the programme was over and all went home.

Caldwell Public Hall in 1969

Main dormitory at Yanco Agricultural High School

Every so often a guy who ran a movie theatre in Wakool came and showed movies which we attended sometimes. I vividly remember one that enthralled me, it was called "Breaking the Sound Barrier".

Sometimes when it was hot we would go for a swim in the dam near our house. Dams in the Riverina were dug by horses pulling scoops and later, in our time, by tractors. They would generally be square big holes, fifteen to twenty metres across, with the scooped out soils put into smoothed piles on each side, ten metres or so back from the hole. These mounds created run off when it rained to send water into the dam. As well a depression or shallow water way across the paddock was directed into the dam for more water access. Around the edge of the water generally was soft mud caused by the hooves of the sheep or cattle as they drank. When we swam however the top metre or so was quite warm, then under that it was very cold, so we had to be careful swimming that we didn't get too cold. The bottom of the dam was very soft mud too so hard to stand on. Hence we didn't swim very often.

Dad and Mum loved gardening and set up large patches of flowers and vegetables. In fact Dad fenced a small area off near a windmill on Tinkler's and grew lots of vegetables. We used to help bottle quantities of vegetables, like carrots, beetroot, tomatoes and beans in Fowlers Vacola jars. He also gave away vegetables to friends and the Baptist minister in Barham when he came to take a church service in the Caldwell hall.

In that generational period it was rare for people to show affection. However Dad and Mum would sometimes walk around the gardens arm in arm. To us three children though, we rarely experienced hugs or kisses or even complimentary words like "I love you" or "thank you". There was always a cold relationship between parents and children. This damaged us for later in life unfortunately.

By this time I began to desire earning money. There was nothing that I would be paid for by the owner on the station and Dad didn't have spare money to pay me so I began collecting drink bottles. There were no cans in those days but plenty of bottles, both clear soft drink and brown beer bottles. In fact motorists and drovers would just toss their empty bottles along the roadsides. So I would ride around the roads and find bottles in the table drains or the grass and carry them home in a bag tied to the handle bar of my bike. I would wash them clean of mud inside and out and when Dad went to Deniliquin he would take them over to North Deniliquin and get money for them. I would get a penny or sometimes if it was special three pence a bottle. The shop he went to was Eli Brown's produce store in Davidson Street. This shop also bought rabbit and hare skins and Dad or I would get money for them too, depending on who caught them initially.

Just over the Edward River Bridge in Deniliquin, on the north side was a track downstream along the river bank. Along this track were several rough derelict shanties made of bags and corrugated iron. Several poor families lived in these and a couple of them were part aboriginals and a couple of them were occupied by drovers between jobs.

In one cottage was a clean living family who were involved in the local Salvation Army Corp. Another of these shanty homes was occupied by a family that had two girls who suffered severe handicaps and I felt sorry for these people. I often wondered what future they all would have. They had no benefits like our family, such as fenced yards, gardens, proper kitchens and lounge rooms and so on.

When I was about 15 Dad showed me how to kill a young sheep for our meat and hang it over night in a cool room to dry and then cut it up. I remember many times crying as I killed it because it was so hard to cut its throat through with a knife and then as I struggled to punch off its woollen skin. It took all my strength and really hurt my hands and knuckles, with no sign of Dad to help, so I just had to keep going until I finished. One had to catch the sheep in a small yard, tip it over, tie its legs together with a rope, take it over in a wheelbarrow to where it was killed and then cut its throat through the wool by bending back its head and using a sharp knife cut its jugular vein (throat). There was a certain procedure to cut and remove the skin (fleece) then take out its innards, remove its head and feet and hang the body in a small gauzed off room at the house.

Another one of my jobs was to lock the calf into a pen each night and milk the cow next morning, then take the milk back to the house, and if plenty, put it through the hand winding separator to take off the cream. Another job was to go down into the timbered parts of our paddocks, generally on Saturdays, and collect thin sticks and put them in piles. Dad would then take the utility down and bring the sticks home to use to light the stove and in winter the open fire in the lounge room.

1956 FLOOD

"STATISTICAL RECORDS since 1914 show that on average every nine years throughout the Riverina it can be expected it will have a less than 10 inch annual rainfall, whilst an over 20 inch rainfall total can be expected every six years". The average annual rainfall over all is 16 ½ inches".[6]

The Darling River joins the Murray River just below Wentworth, north of Mildura. The Darling receives its water from over the Queensland border when the monsoon rains fall in late summer, and flows fairly slowly. However the Murray River receives its water from the Great Dividing Range in winter from heavy rain and in spring from melting snow on the Southern Alps, and flows fairly quickly. In 1956 the La Nina caused heavy rain falls in both river catchments, and the waters met and backed up in the spring.

In the floods of 1956 the waters moved down both river systems for nearly seven months. It has been claimed this to be the biggest flood recorded in the history of the Murray.

There were places where the floodwaters spread up to 100 kilometres wide. It was claimed the flood water covered 7000 square kilometres in the Murray and Murrumbidgee water shed or floodplain. The flood peaked in Deniliquin on Friday 13th July and at Wakool one week later.

After the flood peaked it took several weeks to slowly recede, particularly in the lower river flats and swamps.

For several days Dad and I, with Eric Brookesby, the owner of his three properties, Widgee, Murray Estate and Locksley, went to Widgee. We went in a boat over the floodwaters along the Wakool River flats on Widgee. We saw kangaroos on little

---

6. *Saltbush Country* by John E P Bushby. p. 401. Privately published with the assistance of the Library of Australia History 1980.

knobs starving for food and they would hop out through the water as we approached.

Our main reason for spending those days on the water was to catch and shoot rabbits. There were quite a number of rabbits on logs above the water or in small trees and lignum bushes and they were surrounded by big expanses of muddy water. When we saw a rabbit in a bush ahead of us Eric or Dad would shoot it. Then as we got closer or to other nearby bushes we would see more rabbits. The sound of the rifle would cause all the rabbits in the area to quiver in fear. We could then manoeuvre the boat against each bush and just reach out and pick up the mesmerised rabbits in our hands.

We would ring their necks and leave them in the boat until we later got onto dry land. Then we would skin them to later sell the skins (pellets). We caught several dozen each day for nearly a week. Lignum is a tangled sort of bush that grows mostly in wetter places like swampy areas and areas that occasionally flood. It can be up to two metres high.

Among these lignum bushes where we caught the rabbits by hand were also odd hares, or an occasional rat or snake so we had to be cautious in where we put our hands.

After the 1956 flood the ground was so wet the sheep's hooves became soft and blowflies laid eggs in the moist warm hooves. Then the maggots thrive and the poor sheep suffer pain night and day. The sheep were slowly walked to sheep yards on two of the three properties the Brooksby's owned. There the men pulled every sheep across the shearing shed shearing boards and peeled away all rotting hooves and dug out the maggots with sharp knives.

Then they painted Formalin on the hooves, turned them out into foot baths of Chlorinated Hydrocarbons, such as Dieldrin, for half an hour to kill off the germs and any baby maggots missed. An extreme remedy for an extreme disease. This whole procedure was repeated two weeks later to be sure all sheep had been personally attended to. I might add the smell from the rotting hooves was extremely strong. This month or so of proceedings, involving some 4,000 to 5,000 sheep, was while the Olympic Games were being held in Melbourne, from the 22nd of November to the 8th of December. We listened every day to it on the battery radio as we worked on the sheep in the shearing shed on Locksley. By about the third week working with the sheep I began to get a couple of boils on my arms. After attending a doctor I was told some people are susceptible to the oily sheep's wool or some other thing connected with sheep and to be careful and they will go away. So after lots of pain, lots of puss and bathing they did eventually disappear.

As the year ended I received a letter saying I had failed the Intermediate Certificate. In those times schooling in NSW was called "class" in primary school, so kindergarten, first class, second class etc. Then when in High School it was called "year" so first year, second year and so on up to fifth year. At the end of third year students did the Intermediate Certificate and at fifth year the Leaving Certificate.

THE OUTCOMES OF THIS PERIOD IN MY LIFE

AS I LOOK BACK over the first fifteen years of my life I see some lifelong impressions that have formed my character.

One lasting impression is the sense of the openness of the landscape of the Riverina. I find it so peaceful and serene, like a vast blanket laid over the land as far as the eye can see in every direction. I found this extreme quiet allowed me to think, to talk aloud to myself, or to have my own undisturbed feelings, as though living on a deserted island. No pressure, no arguing or discussion, just choosing what to think and when to act. I believe this experience gave me an amazing sense of oneness with nature and the land. The aborigines always claim the land is their root base and I feel this is part of my Riverina experience.

Another fantastic part of life in the Riverina is the ever changing patterns of living vegetation. From year to year, season to season plants germinate, grow up then die, with many different varieties each year due to the differing climate and rainfall from one season to the next. This ever-changing beauty gives me a sense of awe and wonder at the kaleidoscope of plant life and flowers that appear in no particular order or sequence. They may be prolific in one paddock, or in one area alone, and then the next year there can be no sign of them anywhere. There are also various types of trees that are produced, in many forms and with some of them flowering every so often and others annually.

Quiet flowing waterways and stagnant water holes that are home or headquarters to so many birds, frogs and insects. The sounds these living creatures make are so soft and yet I find them so exhilarating.

However there is also negative aspects across the Riverina plains caused by the effects of man on the environment. The removal of so many trees and the overstocking of vast areas when the country "thrived on the sheep's back". There are also areas of poor soil devoid of minerals and plant life. Scattered across the plains are dried up old water courses with dead and dying trees in them, testifying to a once thriving lifestyle for nature.

I wonder if the trees are asking "where has our life blood gone?" and the answer is silence, as even the leaves have died and gone. There is the carving up of large open paddocks by digging channels, making more fences and roads, more houses and more busy activities, with farmers endeavouring to make more money in less time. The Riverina is changing!

I love to go back and experience all this great Riverina landscape but it also creates an internal struggle. I long to share with the next generation what the land has taught me. To be able to portray a quiet leisurely lifestyle to those who only know speed, instant gratification and the rush of want over need. I'm concerned that they may lose the opportunity to experience the quietness of nature and a meaningful connection to the natural ecosystem in which they live.

I experience so many mixed feelings when I return to my original birthplace.

Finally I have learned to appreciate that God, the Creator of this world and this small section of the landmass of Australia created everything and it was good. For the benefit of mankind He made every aspect of nature and all living things.

www.ingramcontent.com/pod-product-compliance
Lightning Source LLC
Chambersburg PA
CBHW072053290426
44110CB00014B/1663